D0720162

I Saw Heaven!

A Remarkable Visit
to the Spirit World

I Saw Heaven!

A Remarkable Visit to the Spirit World

Lawrence E. Tooley

Fourth Printing: December 1997

International Standard Book Number:

0-88290-599-6

Horizon Publishers' Catalog and Order Number:

1044

Printed and distributed
in the United States of America by

**Horizon
Publishers**

& Distributors, Incorporated

Mailing Address:
P.O. Box 490
Bountiful, Utah 84011-0490

Street Address:
50 South 500 West
Bountiful, Utah 84010

Local Phone: (801) 295-9451
WATS (toll free): 1 (800) 453-0812
FAX: (801) 295-0196

Internet: www.horizonpublishers.com

Dedication

This book is affectionately dedicated . . .

To Georgia, my eternal companion,
whom I have loved since the beginning of time.

To all my children,
whom I have loved through the eternities,
and who have become my intellectual equals,

Lori Gail, Dean Wesley, Nathan Lawrence,
Paul Norman, Lori June
Julie Lynn and Darren Shane.
We have been, and always will be,
eternal friends.

Acknowledgments

I give my heartfelt thanks to God and his representatives beyond the veil for allowing me to return from the spirit world, and for allowing me to remember so vividly my experiences while I was there.

I would like to thank all those that have given me encouragement and helped me to write this book, and also those that have offered me their constructive criticism. I particularly would like to thank Duane S. Crowther and Horizon Publishers, without whose help, expertise and guidance this book might never have been published.

I also want to express my deep appreciation to all those who gave me their professional help, their compassion, and their continuing love and concern as I struggled to recover from my accident. My appreciation is expressed to the plumber that pulled me from the twisted scaffolding at the time of my accident. I was never able to get his name, but without his cool-headed control of the situation at the time, I might never have pulled through.

My special thanks is expressed to Dr. Jay Lynn Smith. Without his remarkable abilities and talents, I wouldn't be able to function physically as well as I do today. I also would like to express my deepest gratitude to the nursing staff at St. Marks hospital for their dedication to duty and for their unwavering attention to my demanding physical needs.

But most important of all, I especially would like to extend and restate my love and appreciation to my wife, Georgia, and to my loving children, for standing by me through the extremely difficult years following the accident. I love them all!

Contents

8 I SAW HEAVEN!

Publisher's Preface

Book publishers are always on the lookout for manuscripts that fit comfortably into their publishing "niche." Here at Horizon Publishers, we're excited when we find materials that lift and inspire, that teach and bring valuable insights to our readers.

Since we have already published several books pertaining to near-death experiences, we were pleased to receive this exciting new work, knowing that it would fit well with what we have already produced. We could see that Larry Tooley's manuscript contained significant new insights that would contribute in a substantial way to the rapidly increasing fund of knowledge concerning life after death.

This brief preface is written to inform you of what happened in the editing process as we prepared the book for publication. To understand our efforts, you need to know a bit about my credentials as editor and publisher of this remarkable book.

I wrote a book entitled *Life Everlasting* three decades ago when my daughter passed away with leukemia. In that book I carefully analyzed evidences of about 150 western pioneers who had been participants in near-death experiences. Their accounts were unique in that they were mostly unpublished—the participants didn't know of what others had seen when they went beyond the veil. I chopped their accounts into little pieces, then compiled those golden nuggets of information into broad patterns, showing that dozens of people had seen the same types of things when they went into the world of spirits.

About a decade after the publication of *Life Everlasting*, near-death experiences were made a subject of everyday conversation across the country as other authors compiled similar experiences. Some competent marketers moved their books to the top of the nation's best-sellers charts, and the type of experiences they wrote about became common knowledge. Since that time, broad patterns of knowledge concerning life after death have been opening up, and the body of knowledge has grown substantially on the subject.

In my own experience, I found myself invited to speak quite frequently on the subject of life after death, and I soon discovered that after I'd finished speaking there would be ten or fifteen people who would gather to share personal or family near-death experiences with me. I'm sure that by now I've heard at least 10,000 such experiences, and I'm very aware that they are as commonplace as they are intriguing.

Near-death experiences come to all kinds of people: men, women, children, people who are very old or very young; people of all different races; atheists and people of all different religious beliefs; people in high stations and people of very humble circumstances. And though the individuals often see things of a heavenly nature, their experiences aren't "sacred"—they usually are being shown around the spirit world and the celestial realms in the same way tourists are exposed to sites when they visit great cathedrals or temples here on earth. There may be things within which are treasured by those of a particular religious persuasion, but those holy things are not usually shared with those who are passing through.

I'm keenly aware that the combined knowledge found in records of their near-death-experience accounts is suitable for comprehensive study and examination, and that those experiences constitute an extremely valuable source of understanding for all who consider them. I'm also aware of the challenges which they pose for scientific examination, and of their limitations as sources of knowledge.

In the experiences I've recorded, I've always sought to be as precise and objective as possible in handling them. Because of this strong desire for accuracy and objectivity, I felt it appropriate to tell you how I, as an editor and publisher, handled Larry Tooley's I Saw Heaven!

After reading over the manuscript, I invited Mr. Tooley and his wife Georgia to come and meet with me. In that interview I probed for details, assuring myself of their validity. I not only talked to Larry and Georgia, I also talked at length with two of their daughters. There's no doubt in my mind that the experience took place and that it's properly recorded.

My next task was to edit the book. I wish to clearly state that I did not ghost write the manuscript. I did not insert new concepts nor ideas, nor my personal beliefs and biases. However, I pressed Larry for more details and for stronger, more exact descriptions of what he saw. Many minor items and descriptions were added by him as a result of those requests. He truly stretched his memory to its limits as he filled in many additional interesting insights. His comment to me was that this effort caused him to relive the experience from beginning to end, and that he was amazed at how vivid his recollections still remain. I sought for the descriptions of places and events to be as complete and definitive as possible. I asked for full names and for dates and places which could be used for verification purposes. As editors do, I touched up the grammar and spelling a bit, and I suggested the rewording of a few sentences for greater clarity, but no major alterations were made to the manuscript.

The most significant change I made, in my editor's role, was to insert subtitles to better identify the many and varied events which the author described. I also broke the book into more chapters to balance chapter lengths, and I worked with the chapter titles to make them more descriptive. The order and flow of the manuscript, however, remained Larry's. My goal was to make the book as informative and "reader friendly" as possible. The book's title, *I Saw Heaven!*, was suggested by Horizon Publishers. I also compiled the extensive conceptual index found at the end of the book.

Here, then, is a careful, accurate description of a very profound, life-changing experience. Larry's insights are broad and varied, and he supplies a substantial number of concepts concerning the next stage of life that will be new and exciting to many readers. We all can learn a great deal from what he saw and reported.

I count it as a privilege to have assisted in the bringing forth of this remarkable book.

Duane S. Crowther
Editor and Publisher

Prologue

T hose who have had near-death experiences will agree with me that we are severely limited by an inadequate vocabulary. A language has not yet been invented that can even begin to describe what they have referred to as "the indescribable."

I have struggled for years trying to find just the right words to convey the beauty, the sights and sounds, and the feelings I experienced on my journey to the other side of the veil.

Within these pages is the fulfillment of that struggle, to bring to light the full extent of my most amazing experience. I have written about the events in this book exactly as I have remembered them, just as they unfolded. It was because of the nature of the accident I was involved in and my sudden return that I have remembered the sequence of events as they happened.

I have begun this book from the earliest memories I have retained. I have not added to, nor deleted anything from my experience.

I only hope you who read this book will find peace and hope within these pages. Those who have gone before are not lost to us. They are only continuing their progression as they wait for us to cross over and catch up to them.

How beautiful and thrilling are the experiences that await each of us when our time comes!

1

The Early Years

I was born early in the morning on the 8th of July, 1942, in Ely, Nevada. I was the youngest one of my family. I have a brother and two sisters who are all at least five years older than I am. This is why I was always known as the baby of the family. World War II was in progress at the time of my birth. I became one of the war babies, the "baby boomers" as we would come to be known.

Two years and three months later, on October 25th, 1944, Georgia followed me into the world. She was the first born in her family, followed by her sister and brother. Her family resided in Magna, Utah, a small mining community nestled in the foothills of the Oquirrh Mountains west of Salt Lake City.

Though we were born only a few hundred miles apart, it would take me almost thirty years to find her.

My family moved a lot in my early years while I was growing up. My mother and father separated while I was quite young. My mother struggled from day to day as she tried to raise four children by herself. We often packed our meager belongings into our old car and headed out following one opportunity after another, but we rarely settled in one place long enough to make friends.

There were four of us kids in my family, but because of our age difference, I was usually left to play by myself. My brother and two sisters had other interests that usually left me out.

Our gypsy lifestyle didn't change much until 1950 when my mother divorced my father and remarried. Our life settled into a routine then as we attempted to grow into a family. We were living in Rangely, Colorado at the time, but economic conditions there forced us to seek something more permanent.

We moved to Durango, Colorado, a beautiful quiet tourist town in southern Colorado at the southern tip of the Rocky Mountains. That was the year I enrolled in the fifth grade. We settled into a large log house at the foot of the local ski slope, in what would later become known as College Heights.

Wendy's Premature Birth and Death

A year later, when I was in the sixth grade, I received the news that my parents were to be blessed with another baby, so it seemed I was going to be known as something other than "the baby of the family." As the weeks slowly passed, I watched with growing interest the expanding condition of my mother's waistline. I hadn't paid particular interest to this event in other women until it became evident in my own mother.

Because of my increased interest, my father decided this was a good time to explain the facts of life to me. A family was living upstairs from us at the time and the mother was pregnant also. She was expecting her fourth child. "Yes," my father said, "She had gotten pregnant the same way that my mother had." For a short time I viewed them both with mixed emotions, but after observing other people in our town and remembering all the other kids in school, I concluded this must be the natural order of things and gave the matter no more thought.

I can remember when the expected day finally arrived. I watched with anticipated interest as my mother and father left for the hospital. Hours later I received a phone call from my dad at the hospital. He told me I had just become a big brother. I now had a little sister.

The next morning my stepfather took me to the hospital with him. I still remember standing at the window of the nursery with my nose pressed against the glass and thinking how small and delicate she was. I watched her two tiny pink fists and squinting eyes and felt very proud that she was my sister. I decided she was going to have the best big brother any girl could ever have. She had been born prematurely. I didn't realize she was struggling and fighting for life.

Her birth certificate read "Wendy Dee." I said her name repeatedly, getting used to it. "My sister, Wendy." Her name seemed to have a magical quality about it.

Early in the morning, the third day after Wendy had been born, my father received a phone call. I could tell immediately by the expression on his face that something was wrong. He put the phone down, and then became very quiet. He stood there for the longest time, finally turning to me with tears in his eyes. He was at a loss for words. Finally, clearing his throat and taking a deep breath, he said the call was from the hospital. Wendy had died early that morning. She was too tiny and fragile to survive. She hadn't been strong enough to hold on.

Our unchecked tears told all that words could not. My turmoil inside finally gave way to an empty, hollow feeling. We had been deprived of this special spirit.

Words cannot possibly convey the loss we felt as we stood in the cemetery on that cold, windblown hillside, watching her tiny casket being lowered into the ground.

Life went on. Slowly, with time, the hurt healed. We found that her memory slowly faded, except on certain occasions when we would gather at her gravesite and remember the sweet, special spirit she was.

I found solace in my solitude as I wandered the hills around Durango. I grew to love the town and the mountains that surrounded it. I was continually drawn into the mountains, seemingly in search of myself.

In the warm spring days before school let out for the summer, I often found myself starring longingly out the open school window. The white puffs of smoke and steam belching from the narrow-gauge train which passed daily from Durango to Silverton and back fascinated me. I was drawn back in time with each signal the engineer gave from the steam whistle, cautioning the local residents at each street crossing as it proceeded north out of town.

The tourist trade supported most of Durango's economy. Therefore, little change occurred while I was growing up. The train was continually crowded with tourists. They each waited their turn for a chance to ride back into history and explore the turn-of-the-century mining town of Silverton. It was still an active mining town and a popular tourist attraction. Little of the town had changed since its heyday.

My grade-school years slipped into Junior High and then into High School. It was in High School that I became acquainted with Larry Talbot. It was interesting to have a friend whose first name was the same as mine. Our activities didn't include each other much at first. It was later, when we began driving and dating, that our paths crossed more frequently. It seemed our relationship grew closer than did that of our other friends. The real bond was still not set. That would wait until our separation from the military, six years later.

I was still in search of something I couldn't find. I grew to be quite a hellion during my last two years in High School. I don't suppose I was much different from a lot of boys growing up at that age. Graduation found me trying my newfound freedom and exerting my independence. As is usually the case, a good solid argument with my parents afforded me the excuse I needed to break away. I joined the navy and was off to explore the world and find myself.

Navy Life and a Stormy Marriage

After graduating from boot camp at San Diego, California in October of 1961, I served a six-month stint at my first duty station, which was at NAS Lemore in California. In November of 1962 they transferred me to Treasure Island for schooling. Treasure Island is a Naval base which they attach to Angel Island. They built it for the 1939 World's Fair, and later it was taken over by the Navy. Angel Island is in the San Francisco Bay, half-way between San Francisco and Oakland.

Night life in San Francisco is enticing. It's intoxicating and keeps calling out for more. I gave in to its temptations. That's when Carol entered my life. Ours was a relationship that was stormy from the beginning. Still, despite our many differences, we married.

Carol had custody of her son, David, from her previous marriage. It wasn't long before I found that marriage and the military don't mix. My long hours away at sea, low pay, and too-few years of experience left little ground on which to build a solid marriage.

Lori Gail was born to us first. She had dark brown hair and dark stormy eyes. They helped to set off her stern, defiant nature. Later, Paul presented himself. He sported blond hair and was a carbon-copy image of me. Still, the children weren't enough to patch up our differences.

During my two-and-a-half years of training reserves in the Navy, I was kept at sea for several weeks at a time. This probably was the reason we stayed married for as long as we did. After they discharged me from the Navy I found civilian life only heightened our differences, driving us even further apart.

It was in January of 1966 that our stormy marriage climaxed. In desperation, I fled from California leaving behind the two things I cherished most in my life then: Lori and Paul. Lori was two-and-a-half years old then and Paul, only a year-and-a-half.

Single Life and College

I returned to Durango and the mountains I loved, and attempted to pick up the pieces of my shattered life. I found some of my high school buddies, who also had joined the Navy, had returned after getting discharged. They were attending Fort Lewis A&M college. They were studying hard and keeping their names at the top of the Dean's Honor list. In the weeks prior to this, I had tried desperately to fill the void in my life from the loss of Lori and Paul. College, it seemed, was a good place to accomplish that.

In the fall of 1966 I enrolled at the college and became a first-year student at the age of twenty-three. The routine of college life helped to heal the hurt in my heart.

A Deep Friendship with Larry Talbot

It was at this time that I found that Larry Talbot, who recently had been discharged from the Marines, was now back home. He was working for one of the local florists in town. I looked him up, eager to renew old acquaintances and to have a close friend—I needed someone to pal around with.

I learned he had the honor and distinction of being the shortest Marine, at 5 foot 3 inches tall, ever to have successfully served a four-year hitch.

It wasn't long before we became close friends. I included him in everything I did. We both shared a certain sense of freedom and found our interests were mutual. College life afforded us quite a variety of dating opportunities as we sampled the flavor of the local female population.

I came to realize just how height-conscious Larry really was. He seemed to think his short height afforded him little opportunity to succeed in life. There had been more than one opportunity for me to bolster his spirits. Some nights after dropping our dates off, we found ourselves parked, philosophizing on the outcome of our dates and on life in general. It was on occasions such as these that I found his spirits to have sunk as low as he pictured his height to be.

Many nights we sat talking until three or four in the morning, finally stopping when I felt he was more inspired about the future and a bit more secure in how he felt about himself.

I developed an interest in the early history of Colorado and the Durango area after running across several books in the college library. They detailed the exploration of the Spanish and their discovery of gold in the southwest regions of Colorado. We tramped the hills and mountains around Durango as we fancied ourselves to be daring treasure hunters.

A search of the local records and archives at the library convinced us that we were on the track of a fabulous lost Spanish treasure buried somewhere in the mountains near Pagosa Springs. Pagosa Springs is a small town near the base of Wolf Creek Pass, which is about 50 miles to the east of Durango.

We spent several weekends there and were convinced that we were close to a historic find. We outfitted ourselves with gear we felt we needed to tramp the hills in search of our treasure. We bought canteens, rope, flashlights, and anything else we could think of. Larry convinced me it would be better if we were to keep all the supplies in his room.

It was shortly after this I learned he had devised a method by which he felt he could stretch himself in hopes of adding a few inches and making himself taller. Above the door which opened into his room from the hall was a tram window, an item that is quite popular in older hotels. He had fashioned a hangman's noose from the rope in our supplies. He would hook the rope into the top of the tram window, letting the noose hang just below the sill of the door. Then, while standing on a chair, he would slip the noose under his chin and slowly lower himself off the chair until the rope supported his full weight. Larry felt ten to fifteen minutes a day in this position would stretch himself.

I became alarmed and frightened when I found out what he was doing. His depression each time we talked troubled me. I had never met anyone before who was struggling with depression like he was. I grew increasingly frustrated and worried each time we got into a discussion and I found him depressed again. Each time, I tried to encourage and convince him there wasn't anything wrong with his height, but the next time was always worse than the time before.

My anxiety welled up inside me each time I thought about his deepening depression and his trying to stretch himself with the rope. I couldn't shake the feeling something unfortunate was going to happen.

We both knew that winter would soon settle into the mountains. We made plans for the following weekend to go in search of our treasure one last time that year.

We went on a date that Saturday night, taking our girlfriends out on the town. After a gourmet dinner, we topped the evening off by watching the moon rise over the mountains from College Heights. I felt it was the end to a perfect night as we dropped our dates off, but Larry apparently did not.

Larry and I reviewed the evening over a cup of coffee. This time he was more withdrawn, more distant. He seemed barely able to lift his spirits off the floor. Not dropping his guard for a second, he had succeeded in putting on quite a front for the girls, but I knew differently.

I had never seen him this low or despondent. I was afraid to leave him alone. It was four that Sunday morning before I felt I was finally able to leave him. He had finally committed himself to some long-range goals. I hoped I had finally instilled some sense of direction in him. Nevertheless, I still couldn't shake my feeling of concern for him as I drove home.

Larry Talbot's Unfortunate Death

We had agreed I would pick him up about 11 o'clock that same morning for breakfast. It was 10:55 when I walked down the hall and stopped in front of his room. The cracked and faded paint of the number "23" peeked through from the past mirroring the age of the hotel. I knocked, waiting for a reply. The Sunday morning stillness filled the air. Maybe he just slept in, I thought as I knocked again, louder. There still was no answer. I checked my watch. Yes, I was on time. Where was he? He knew I was coming by for him. I noticed the tram window above his door was closed as I knocked the third time.

Strange, I thought. That's not like him. He always leaves it open. I went down the hall to the lobby to see if his key was in the key box. Normally, he would leave his door key at the office if he went out. It was gone. I knew he had to be in the hotel somewhere.

After checking the usual places and not finding him, I went back to his room. This time I pounded on the door with the flat of my hand. I wanted to make sure he wasn't asleep. There still was no answer.

I figured he probably had just stepped out and forgot to leave his key this time, and yet he knew I was supposed to pick him up that morning. I checked back several times during the day, finding conditions to be the same as I had found them earlier. A vague uneasiness nagged at me as I retired for the night. I was disappointed that I had missed him all that day.

It was 10 o'clock the next day when my boss told me I had a phone call. After answering it I found it was Nancy, Larry's date from Saturday night. Her voice quivered when she asked if I had heard the news. I told her I hadn't and wanted to know what news, thinking it strange that she would be calling me at work. Her choking words failed to prepare me for what she was about to tell me.

I was stunned, unable to speak when she told me Larry Talbot had been found dead in his room that morning. In shock, I became vaguely aware that she was calling my name.

"Larry? Larry? Are you there?"

I stammered, trying to find my voice. "How did it happen?" I wanted to know. Was my worst fear about to be realized? I didn't want to hear the words, but I had to know.

She said that when he hadn't reported for work this morning, his boss had become worried. This was out of character for him. They called around to his friends, finally calling the hotel manager asking if he would check his room. When the manager couldn't raise an answer from inside, he let himself in with his pass key. That was when they found Larry, slumped against the door.

Since I was the last to see him alive, she told me the police were looking for me for questioning. My thoughts were jumbled and confused. I found it hard to focus my attention as I related to my boss why I had to leave and what had happened. He told me to take my time and offered his help if he could do anything.

I grabbed my coat as I stumbled through the door, letting it close behind me. I felt defeated, as if I had somehow failed to prevent something like this from happening. Yes, my worst fears had come true. How could I have not known something was wrong? How could I have let this happen?

I was still beside myself when I reported to the police station. The detective handling the case ushered me into his office. As he sat across the desk from me, he kept looking at some pictures he was holding while he questioned me. As I related everything concerning that Saturday night, he took notes.

A police officer stuck his head through the door. He interrupted us to tell the detective they wanted him out front for a moment. As he excused himself and left the room, he laid the pictures on his desk. I couldn't resist peeking as I rose in my seat so I could see the pictures.

The top picture showed Larry, slumped almost to the floor, his hands between his knees, leaning against the door. The rope around his neck was still hooked into the top of the tram window. The realization of what happened hit me.

I asked what they had found when the detective returned. He said they had found a bump on the back of his head and that he had died of strangulation.

I asked him if he thought it was suicide. It appeared to be, but the bump on the back of his head didn't figure in. "No," he said. "Because of the evidence, we're treating it as an accident."

I knew then he had tried one time too many to stretch himself. Apparently, after leaving him that morning, he had attempted to stretch himself again. Setting everything into place as he had before, he stood on the chair and hooked the rope into the top of the tram window. After he had placed the noose under his chin, he became unbalanced, causing the chair to flip out from under him. He had fallen back, hitting his head against the door and knocked himself unconscious. When he slumped forward, the noose slipped over his head and cut off his air, strangling him. The nylon rope had stretched because of his weight, letting him sag almost to a sitting position against the door.

I had grown so close to him, and now he was gone from my life. I asked if I could see him, but the detective advised against it. He said it would be too difficult and would be better to wait until the funeral. I knew I had to do something or I would go crazy thinking about it. I went to see his family and asked if I could speak at his funeral. His mother questioned me about what I thought had happened. I told her what the detective had told me about it being an accident, but I couldn't bring myself to tell her about his periods of depression and despondency. I felt I needed to protect her from any speculation and any more pain. His mother knew we had gotten to be best friends the last few months and agreed to let me speak. She was grateful that someone who cared so much would be able to speak for Larry and she thanked me.

While writing Larry's memorial, I struggled with my emotions as I tried to condense his life into a few words on a piece of paper. I knew I needed help and someone to talk to. I called Nancy and asked her if we could meet that night. I was grateful and relieved when she said yes.

I drove aimlessly that afternoon, completely lost in my thoughts and emotions. I struggled through my tears to make some sense out of what had happened. I had regained some composure by the time I knocked on her door that night, but I still couldn't control my shaking hands.

We struggled to make conversation, avoiding the issue as we drove to a secluded spot. Shutting off the ignition, we sat there in silence for a long time as we stared blankly out the window. When I finally turned to face Nancy and our eyes met, I could see a pale glow reflecting off the tears trickling down her face. My pain and heartache mirrored the expression I saw in her eyes.

I kept telling myself Nancy needed reassurance and comforting also. She looked pleadingly into my eyes as she whispered, "Why Larry? Why does it have to be this way? Why did he have to die so young?"

"I don't know," I murmured.

I pulled the paper from my pocket that I had been writing my talk on and tried to read it to her. It sounded awkward and hollow and was a pitiful expression of what I was really feeling. She said she understood, and she offered some suggestions. It was, after all, my choice. I was the only one who really knew what Larry thought and felt. She said when the time was right I would be able to express what I felt. I would be O.K.

I fought back the tears that morning as I stood before the podium looking out at the people who had gathered. My voice quivered as I tried, through blurry eyes, to read my notes. The papers rattled as my hand shook, falling to the floor. I realized trying to read them was no good. I looked down at Larry and my heart pounded. I could almost see him move, but as I blinked away the tears I knew I was only seeing things. He wasn't going to move, ever again, and I kept thinking—why Larry, why?

As Nancy had said, at the right time I would find the words I was looking for. This time, I spoke from my heart and not from a prepared text as I told them of a side of Larry no one knew but me. The words were choked out, venting part of my frustration and draining some of my pent-up rage.

Afterwards, I escorted Larry's coffin as the pall bearers carried the casket to the cemetery where we laid to rest his hopes and dreams on that same hillside slope where twelve years before we had buried Wendy and our hopes and dreams.

Travels and a Move to Salt Lake City

During the next four years I grappled with my life, still looking for meaning and direction. The struggle took me from Colorado to Illinois to Florida and back. Still, I couldn't find what I was looking for.

It was in the spring of 1971 that I felt the need to travel again. I felt that I would like to see South Dakota, but Salt Lake City seemed to draw me. My two sisters lived there, and I used the excuse that I wanted to visit with them on my way through. Once there, I felt inexorably held, unable to leave.

2

Marrying Georgia

An Unusual Attraction:
Hidden Memories Stirred

In June, 1971, I was residing at a boarding house in downtown Salt Lake City. One night, while I was cleaning and doing my laundry, I was listening to the radio. I became dissatisfied with my usual broadcast station and began changing the setting of the dial, eventually coming to rest upon a station that carried the widely heard and discussed "Public Pulse." This immediately satisfied my desire, which I found highly unusual, for commentary type broadcasts generally bored me to death.

I heard the announcer say that a special guest speaker who said she was a representative of a movement called The Inner Peace Movement would soon be speaking. Her specialty ran deep into the realm of extrasensory perception. I found my interest highly aroused. I paid particular attention to her discourse on the subject, relating many of the things she said with experiences of my own.

Several times I heard her say that they would conduct a meeting for all interested persons at the World Motel on a particular evening the following week. I decided I would attend to find out for myself if what she said was true or if she were an elaborate fake. If possible, I hoped to enhance my own knowledge of the subject.

The evening for the meeting came and as usual, I was early. I dislike being late for appointments or meetings of any kind. Because of this, I could be found pacing or wandering the floor as much as half an hour early.

This evening proved to be no exception; I was one of the first few through the door. By chance, I happened to sit near the middle of the room, half way from the front and to the right of the center isle.

Sometime before the start of the meeting, a man and woman made their entrance and seated themselves just to my right and several rows ahead of me.

My first impression was that they were married. Despite this, I felt a certain attraction to the woman. Through the presentation, I found I could not keep my eyes off her. She sensed that someone was staring at her, but when she turned to see whom it was, I would have my eyes riveted on the speaker.

It didn't take me long to discern that they weren't married and that they certainly were not brother and sister. My impression was that they were at most, close friends.

When the meeting closed, I was talking to one of the members of the audience when the woman approached us. She stood before us, waiting patiently for me to finish what I was saying. I found myself gazing into crystal-clear, emerald-green eyes. Hidden memories nudged my consciousness as deep-seated feelings stirred, begging for recognition. I felt certain I knew her.

As we chatted, I found myself inviting her to a social affair to which I had received an invitation. She accepted without hesitation. I then invited her for a bite to eat in the motel's coffee shop.

During our discussion, I found that I seemed to possess certain knowledge about her. She was amazed with the tidbits of knowledge which I revealed to her. It was as if I were simply hearing a confirmation of what I already knew to be true. Within a few short hours we revealed our life histories to each other. Because of our backgrounds, we both closely resembled each other's ex-spouses, which caused both of us a certain uneasiness.

Yet, there was a definite familiarity that was soon to become crystal clear.

Strangely enough, my actions seemed to be perfectly directed as if they were predestined. A rekindling of an old love which was spawned somewhere before the dawning of creation seemed more likely to be the birthplace of such actions.

Though neither of us had been fully active in our church participation during the years of our previous marriages, we both had a strong desire to start off our relationship together as active, participating church goers. When we first met and I found that Georgia was a member of my church, our second date had been to attend church together that next Sunday. I knew she hadn't believed I was serious about going to church so that next Sunday morning I was ringing her doorbell two hours before church was to begin. She expressed total surprise when she opened the door and found me standing there smiling, dressed for church. I offered to bathe the kids and dress them in their Sunday best while she dressed.

What a proud group we made as we walked hand in hand into church that morning. After that, church became a regular occasion for us each Sunday. It was after our fourth date and I had proposed to Georgia for the first time that we began attending the temple-preparation classes held every Sunday evening. It had taken us three months to complete the classes and now we had only to wait for the required time to pass. The time seemed to drag on at a snail's pace.

As the weeks passed, I became more determined in my courtship and I proposed marriage several times. She expressed concern whether I would be able to accept her two children. Here too, I found an unknown familiarity as I strove to become acquainted with them.

Each time I held her close and peered into her eyes, hidden feelings stirred within the depths of my soul. I slowly overcame each of her objections as I courted her, occupying her every waking moment.

Because of her tragic first marriage, gaining her trust was not easy. She put me through one test after another. My offhanded remarks to her veiled questions were sometimes misinterpreted, and each perceived wrong answer caused me to lose ground. Each time as I realized how my answers affected her I would have to restate those answers to put her fears to rest. If she were to accept my proposals, she had to be sure she wouldn't be repeating the mistakes of the past.

Finally, she relented and accepted my proposal. It was without hesitation that we set the date for November 20, 1971. Love between us seemed boundless, fresh and new. We could hardly wait for each passing day so that we could spend our available hours together. Our love's euphoric glow transcended time and space as each shared experience seemed to evoke a continuation of a past relationship.

Though a careless gaiety fronted her every action, a deep worry sometimes clouded her eyes and masked her emotions. Yet, as seen through my eyes, she had the true gracefulness and beauty with which she was created.

Georgia's Account of the Courtship

I was just bringing a painful chapter of my life to close. I was legally separated and had filed for divorce from my very unhappy eight-year marriage. Men were the last thing on my mind. If anything, I only wanted to use men the way I had been used. But right now all I wanted was freedom to do what I wanted, when I wanted, without retaliation from a demanding, demeaning tyrant of a husband. Peace, quiet, and the seclusion of my small apartment with Nathan and Lori, my two children, was all I really wanted.

Kim, a very good friend whom I had grown up with, had been keeping tabs on me since I had filed for divorce. He seemed to think I needed to get out and meet new people, and he kept telling me it wasn't good to stay cooped up in my apartment all the time.

There was a group meeting in Salt Lake City that he said would be fun to go listen to. He said that getting out among the living would help me get over my divorce quicker. No matter how much I objected, he only argued that much harder. Finally, to shut him up, I agreed to go. His sister agreed to babysit for us that night as he picked me up.

Although we were only a few minutes early when we arrived, we still had our pick of some very good seats as we filed in with the rest of the people showing up for the meeting. Everyone quieted down as the guest speaker was introduced.

It wasn't long before I became aware I was being watched. I looked over the people at the meeting, but no one seemed to be paying much attention to me. I couldn't get over the feeling of being watched, but every time I looked behind me, everyone appeared to be watching the speaker.

One guy in particular caught my attention. Though he was never looking at me when I turned around, my attention was always drawn to him. He was very good-looking. I had noticed another man though, whom I recognized from other meetings I had gone to. When the meeting ended, I asked Kim to wait. I wanted to talk to some people before we left and went looking for the man I recognized earlier. It was a good thing, because Kim had seen another girl he wanted to talk to.

When I found my old acquaintance, he was talking to the man I thought was so good-looking. As I walked up to them, he kept looking back and forth between me and my old friend. I can't explain why I was so attracted to him at first, unless it was the way he kept looking into my eyes as if he couldn't take his gaze from mine. When they stopped talking, it gave me a chance to talk to my friend. But every time I looked at him it was like he was transfixed with my eyes.

Our conversation quickly centered on the two of us as my friend left. He introduced himself as Larry and I told him my name was Georgia. When he offered to buy me something to eat in the coffee shop I immediately said yes. I had almost forgotten about Kim. Being with Larry seemed like the most natural thing in the world right then.

We laughed and talked about many things, and I was enjoying being with him. When he asked if I would like to go for a ride in his Cadillac I said Sure, why not. I should have been afraid to go with someone I'd never known before, but somehow it all seemed perfectly natural.

Then I remembered Kim and wondered what he must be thinking of me. I told Larry I had come with my friend and that I would have to ride home with him. Larry didn't waste any time offering to give me a ride home. I told him I would have to ask Kim first. When I found Kim, he was relieved that I had a ride home since he had found a cute little blond and wanted to get acquainted with her.

As I look back now, I find it ironic that we went to the meeting with each other but left with someone else. As Larry and I left the coffee shop, I was expecting this big fancy car. Instead, he led me to an old 1962 Chevy. When I ask him about his Cadillac he remarked he had only been kidding.

I'll never know what possessed me to start talking about my life that night. We drove around for hours talking about our past. He asked me what my sign was and when I told him I was a Scorpio, I thought he was going to jump out of the car. This made me curious so I asked him what his sign was. I almost jumped out of the car then. When I learned he was a Cancer and he found out I was a Scorpio it was like we had suddenly developed the plague. We couldn't sit any further apart than if we had been at either end of a Greyhound bus. Larry's ex-wife was a Scorpio and my ex-husband was a Cancer.

It was four in the morning when Larry finally drove me home. By then our chill had defrosted as we became more familiar with each other. It seemed strange that he seemed to know so much about me. When he asked me to go to the Lucky Club with him the next Wednesday night, I accepted. That was our first date.

That Wednesday while we were dancing, the conversation turned to what religion we were. When I told him I was a member of the LDS church he smiled as he told me he was a member also. When the dance ended, Larry was very quiet for a while. Then he asked me if I would like to go to church the next Sunday. I didn't know whether to believe him or not but decided to take a chance. Although I had been born and raised in the church, the strain I was under in my first marriage had kept me inactive. It was a refreshing change of pace to be invited to church. I'm not sure I really took him seriously, especially when he told me that he was also inactive. People don't usually make dates for church very often.

I was really surprised when I answered the door early that Sunday morning. Larry was standing there dressed in a suit, ready for church. His appreciative smile of me standing in the door in my pajamas told me he was serious in more ways than one. I couldn't believe it when he told me he would help get Nathan and Lori ready for church if I wanted to get dressed. It was really nice walking into church arm in arm that morning. Church became a regular function for us after that.

Larry began proposing to me almost from the beginning. I was very cautious and didn't want to jump back into another disastrous relationship so soon after my divorce. Every time he would ask, I would say no. He even started asking my friends how he could get me to say yes. I put him through one test after another. If he had failed even one of them, I would have kissed him off.

In September we went to San Diego with some of our friends. We managed to slip off by ourselves for dinner the second night we were there. It was a romantic candlelight dinner by the ocean when he proposed to me again. I finally said yes. Later that night he pulled the tab off a pop can and slipped it onto my finger. He said this would make it official until he could afford to give me a real ring.

It would have been so easy to have stopped off in Las Vegas on the way back and gotten married, but we had to wait for my divorce to become final. We set the date for November the 20th.

I can still remember how embarrassed we were on the day of the wedding. People I had known all my life were there, and yet I couldn't face them. Our little family made quite a sight that day. I was dressed in a purple mini skirt with white boots and my hair had been permed and piled on top of my head. Larry was so handsome dressed in his suit.

We had bought Nathan a brand-new suit for the wedding. He tore the knee out of the pants jumping off my mother's front porch after the wedding. Lori was dressed in her own little purple mini skirt and white boots to match mine. The kids were so excited they couldn't sit still for a minute.

As we stood before the bishop that afternoon waiting to say "I do," I thought we were both going to faint. I don't think anyone but the bishop heard us say "I do."

Larry's Foreknowledge: Expecting Twins

It was our wedding day and I could hardly wait to make Georgia mine. We were both painfully shy and embarrassed as the hour drew nigh. We were so shy we couldn't face the friends and relatives that had gathered until the appointed hour found us ready to exchange our vows.

Here, seemingly, my search had ended. I'd found what I had been looking for all my life. At first, ours seemed like a fairy tale marriage. We could hardly stand to be away from each other. It wasn't long though, before reality set in.

Because of my work schedule, we delayed our honeymoon for two weeks. We had arranged to spend our honeymoon in Las Vegas. Georgia's mother had agreed to watch Nathan and Lori for us.

After arriving in Las Vegas, we settled ourselves into our room and set about making reservations to see the Ann-Margaret show and arranged for our first, festive honeymoon dinner. We had refreshed ourselves with a hot shower, deciding a short nap was in order before we began our evening.

Our expectations and preparations soon faded. Georgia began feeling sick, too sick in fact to even get out of bed. As sick as she was feeling, she felt worse thinking I might miss the Ann-Margaret show and wanted me to go anyway. I couldn't leave knowing how sick she was.

Instead of the elaborate first honeymoon dinner we had planned, I ordered a pizza and salad instead, which we shared in our room, Georgia confined to bed and me consoling her. I still remember how upset she had become because she thought she had ruined our special weekend.

This small triviality hadn't bothered me. I had sensed an underlying feeling behind her sickness which was born out several weeks later by her actions.

When I was sure of what was happening, I surprised her when I announced she was pregnant. She seemed almost to be in shock. "I couldn't be," she said with deep concern. Her last doctor had told her, after Lori was born, that another pregnancy could be very dangerous. She might even lose her life because of it. Somehow, I knew better.

Finally at my insistence, Georgia set a doctor's appointment. She was very excited afterwards when she came home, eager to share the news.

Yes! She was pregnant, just as I had insisted. She wanted to know how I had known. Again, she expressed her concern because of her previous doctor's warning. I grasped the opportunity of the moment.

"Don't worry," I said. "I know everything will be just fine." I felt my mind opening up. I was very sure about the information that was coming through to me. "You'll have a few problems along the way," I said reassuringly, "but nothing serious will prevent you from having the babies."

She looked apprehensive at me, "What babies?" she asked.

I looked into her eyes reassuringly. "Let me explain," I said, taking a deep breath. "Remember when I said you were pregnant? I didn't tell you everything."

I hesitated, not sure of the reaction I would get. "Not only are you pregnant, but you're going to have twins."

Shocked, Georgia almost fell out of her chair. "You're crazy," she cried. "I can't have twins. I'm not even supposed to have one."

I took her in my arms, trying to soothe her. "I know honey, but it still doesn't change things. You're still going to have twins. I'm not sure what the reason is, but you're going to have them. God knows what he's doing."

"What reason?" she asked, pulling away from me to sit down.

"At this point I'm not sure. I can tell you they'll be a boy and a girl," I went on to explain. "They'll be as different as night and day. The boy will be all boy and the girl will be all girl, small and petite." I didn't wait for her stunned reaction. "Complications will set in while they're being born. The girl will be just fine, but they'll almost lose the boy, but at the last minute they'll save him."

Georgia looked at me incredulously as I went on to explain several other things that would happen, including the date and the time I thought they would be born.

She still looked at me, not knowing whether to believe me or not. Still, I was firm in my convictions, convinced in the knowledge of what I was saying.

My words must still have echoed in her mind when she went for her next appointment. She had asked her mother to go along. It must have been more for moral support than anything else.

"Everything's progressing just fine," the doctor reported. "There's nothing to worry about."

Hesitantly, Georgia asked, "Do you think I could possibly be having twins?"

The doctor looked at her, puzzled. "I don't know. Why do you ask?"

"It just seems I'm getting bigger, faster than I did with my other two. Besides," she added, "my husband thinks I might be having twins."

"Well, let's take another look," he said.

Sure enough, there they were. Two distinct heart beats. Shock set in as Georgia realized that I was right, but how could I be? she thought. This was not supposed to be happening. She had been warned about having another one, and now she was having two! How was it going to be possible?

As they left the office that morning, Georgia told her mother what the doctor had said. She sagged against the wall in shock and disbelief. Yet, the evidence was irrefutable. When she came home and told me, I just smiled.

"But how did you know?" she demanded.

"I just know," I said simply and smiled. I wasn't sure how I had known myself, let alone how I should try to explain it. Yet, the knowledge was just there, as it had been the day I had looked into her beautiful green eyes and realized that I had known her before. Somewhere, deep within, she stirred powerful, familiar feelings. Fleeting memories were nudged to life, and yet they remained elusive.

Her pregnancy was not totally without its problems, though. The day she excitedly announced she was pregnant, I also had to explain that I had lost my job. It didn't take me long to land another job. I hired on with Atlas Electric, a fast-growing, progressive electrical contracting firm.

Georgia contracted the Hong Kong flu several weeks after becoming pregnant, which confined her to bed for the next couple of months. She grew extremely weak and unable to eat. Fever blisters covered her throat and mouth, making it very difficult for her to eat even the simplest things. I spent hours sitting on the bed, letting popsicles drip between her swollen lips.

Because I was unable to give her all the care she needed, Georgia's mother bundled her and the two children up and took them to her house. The days passed slowly as she was gradually nursed back to health. Everything then seemed to confirm her former doctor's warning.

In her fourth month, her doctor ordered her to bed to keep from aborting the twins. For Georgia it was a bitter contradiction, but she followed his orders. Many time the contractions would be so strong she couldn't move. This was especially so if we went anywhere in the car. Sometimes I would have to wait ten minutes or more for the contractions to subside so she could get out of the car.

Events Moving to a Climax

After we were first married, we moved into Georgia's apartment in Magna, just west of Salt Lake City. We soon felt it was too small and moved into a nice two-bedroom apartment complex in nearby Taylorsville. At first it was just the right size. Nathan and Lori shared the one bedroom and Georgia and I the other. We both knew that once the twins were born, they would all have to share the same room, a situation that would soon get out of control.

The firm I was working for at the time was wiring new homes for a contractor in Midvale. I had become pretty well acquainted with him and liked the homes he was building. Georgia and I checked with the bank and found that I had been in Utah long enough to qualify for a home loan. At six months, Georgia was already looking full term. We knew we didn't have much time left.

We immediately started loan proceedings on a small red-brick rambler. The home we had chosen was progressing nicely and we visited it on a regular basis. After meeting Georgia, the General Contractor took a special interest in us. He had a car phone in his truck, which he always parked on the job. He could see how anxious I was becoming with each passing day. He agreed if a call should come through from Georgia, he would contact me if I were anywhere on his project. This made it easier for me, but still didn't lessen the anxiety that was building within me. My concern was becoming very evident whenever his phone would sound off. My pulse would race wildly and I would almost race him for it.

Everything was rushing to a climax: the completion of our first home, the finalization of our loan, the birth of the twins and the date of our temple marriage.

Because of the rules of our Church, when we were married before in a civil ceremony, we knew we would have to wait one year before we could be married in the temple. Even before we had gotten married, Georgia and I had been attending church on a regular basis and had even completed all our temple-preparation classes.

3

The Birth of the Twins

It was Tuesday morning, the 5th of July, 1972 when Georgia announced she had gone into labor. The babies were coming six weeks prematurely. I called my boss, telling him I couldn't make it to work that morning. Excitement gripped me as I loaded her suitcase into the back seat. I led her gingerly to the car and helped her settle into the front seat. I had a bad case of the jitters as we started for the hospital. At first, Holy Cross Hospital, in Salt Lake City, hadn't seemed so far away, but her pains were increasing in frequency. I was beginning to wonder if we would make it on time.

"You'd better hurry," she would gasp between breaths. "Oh! Oh! Slow down," she grimaced in pain. "Take it easy on the bumps."

I'd slow the car to a reasonable speed as she had requested. Then another contraction would hit. "Hurry," she would gasp.

Again, I'd gun the car forward. Georgia gripped the car door as we pulled up in front of the hospital. "Let's go home. I can't go through with it," she panted. "I've changed my mind."

"Oh no you don't" I said, taking her by the arm as I opened the car door. "We're not backing out now."

She reluctantly let me lead her through the door. This was the start of her 56-hour ordeal. For the next fifty-six hours, to compensate for my feelings of total helplessness and inadequacy, I sat by her bed giving her ice chips and tried to help her with each contraction.

We had arranged with the doctor so that I could be present during the delivery. Late Thursday afternoon on the 7th, things hadn't changed. I was only kidding her as I said, "Honey, if you could just wait a few more hours, they'd be born on my birthday."

She didn't say anything. She didn't have to—the wilting looks she gave me said it all. Finally, about eight that evening, they said she was ready and wheeled her into the delivery room. She had given me her glasses to hold for her until it came time for the delivery. I was to give them to her then so she could see everything that happened. Without them, everything would be just a blur.

I quickly put on the delivery room clothing I was given and rushed to the swinging door leading into delivery room. I didn't know if I could just walk in or not, so I stood there with Georgia's glasses, waiting for someone to say it was O.K. As I looked, I could see a flurry of activity through the crack between the swinging doors.

The pain had become unbearable for Georgia. Fifty-six hours of labor had drained her strength, and now the stress of the delivery made it feel as if her insides were being crushed. "I can't stand the pain any longer," she weakly uttered.

Georgia's Brief Glimpse of Delivery From Outside Her Body

Georgia later described to me what happened to her next. A soothing calm and tranquility swept over her as the pain vanished. She was watching the delivery from a detached position above the bed and to one side. How wonderful to be out of the pain, she thought to herself.

Her immediate impulse was to leave. She had never experienced such warmth and overwhelming love before. There was such a sense of peace and joy. She looked again at herself lying on the bed and realized the twins needed her help to be born, even just to live.

Difficult Deliveries

Suddenly she was back in her body. As her overpowering emotions climaxed, the pain flooded over her in cascading waves. She raised her head as Julie protested her expulsion into this harsh environment.

Where is he? she kept wondering. The babies are being born and he isn't here. I need my glasses. Everything's just a blur.

It was 8:56 P.M. when I heard Julie cry. I was thrilled. I anxiously peered through the crack trying to get a glimpse of anything, but all I could see were the doctor's clothes covered with blood. I was riveted to the spot. I desperately wanted to go in but was restrained by my emotions.

Suddenly, the doors swung open and a nurse rushed through with a bundle cradled in her arms. "Are you the father?" she asked, stopping as she saw me.

"Yes, I am," I stammered.

She turned the little bundle, carefully pulling the blankets back so I could see. "You've got a beautiful daughter."

Poor Julie. She really looked like she had been through the war. "Would you like to go to the nursery with me?" she asked as she smiled reassuringly to me.

I wanted to more than anything right then but I knew I had to stay. "I can't," I said. "I've got one more coming." The nurse quickly turned and disappeared down the hall before I could ask her if I could go in.

Those inside had no time to worry about me standing outside the doors. They suddenly had a crisis on their hands. Darren was in trouble. They were losing him and had to get him out fast. Georgia kept slipping in and out of consciousness, dimly aware of their frantic communications.

"Quick, we're losing him. Nurse! Give her another shot. We've got no time to lose," the doctor said as Darren's heart stopped. They fought frantically to get him out. Every second was precious.

It was 9:14 P.M. when the doctor received a weak cry from Darren in response to his efforts. Relieved, he handed him to the nurse and bent to the task of completing the process with Georgia. There still were precise precautions to be completed before everyone was out of danger.

I beamed with pride and satisfaction as I looked at the weary little baby the nurse presented to me as she pushed open the doors. "We almost lost him," she said, "but everything's just fine now. He's going to be O.K. What a handsome young man he is."

I asked how Georgia was. "She's weak. They just wheeled her into recovery in the next room. You can go in and see her."

I wiped tears of gratitude from my eyes as I held Georgia's hand and kissed her. "I love you very much. Thank you for a beautiful set of twins. What a wonderful birthday present you've given me!" I held her, talking softly to her. I was elated and on such an emotional high I could hardly contain myself.

"You had my glasses. I could hardly see a thing. Where were you?"

"You've got them now," was my weak response. I felt guilty for not being in there, but it was all over now and everyone was safe. As I looked into her heavy leaden eyes, I knew what an ordeal she'd been through. What she needed now was sleep and recuperation. I was exhausted too. I kissed her goodbye and stopped by the nursery one last time before going home.

I had been right about everything. Everything that is, except the hour and the exact date they were born. Still, not a bad track record. At least with my forewarnings and with Georgia prompting the doctor about her medical history, they averted disaster.

Move to the New Home

I was as proud as a peacock the day we brought them home from the hospital. The twins were so small both fit into the bassinet I had placed in the back seat. They still had room to spare.

Three weeks later, with all four children crowded into the one bedroom of our apartment, our house was finally finished. It was not a moment too soon. We welcomed the relief. Having all four children in one bedroom made for extremely crowded conditions.

Although our loan was not ready to close yet, the contractor felt sorry for us and agreed to let us move in early. Three weeks later, when we closed the loan, we were pretty well settled. That was on the 18th of September, 1972. The twins had just turned eight weeks old.

4

The Accident

D uring the month before we moved into our new home, I was working on a warehouse at 20 East Union Avenue in North Salt Lake City. It was across the street from United Van Lines. The company that had bought the building was converting it into a factory to build modular homes and condominiums. My job was to install the required electrical wiring and outlets. Because of the nature of the reconstruction, most of the work had to be done from a rolling scaffold.

By the time we moved into our house, I had completed the installation of the lighting and the required outlets. All that remained was to hook up a thirty-horsepower compressor. The electrical panel we fed the compressor from was found near the front door of the building in the corner. The compressor was at the opposite end of the warehouse, approximately 130 feet away. Because of the distance involved, I had to install a junction box at the midway point. I only needed another day and I would be finished, just in time for the weekend.

Georgia's Strong Foreboding

That night, preparing for bed, Georgia and I had been talking about how the closing of the house had gone. The subject eventually changed to the job I was on and how things were going.

"Are you about finished with it?" she asked.

"I'll be able to finish it tomorrow."

"What have you got left?"

"The only thing I've got left to do is hook up a compressor," I said.

"How long is it going to take?"

"I should be finished with it in the afternoon. We have to wait until lunch for the office personnel to leave so I can kill the power to the panel. We have to pull wire into the panel, and then hook it up."

"Is it dangerous?" she asked.

"No," I said. "That's why I turn off the power. This isn't something I can do while it's hot."

"Are you going to have some help?" she asked with concern.

"Yeah," I said. "I have a helper. He'll be on the scaffold as we pull the wire in and I'll be on the ground at the panel."

"What scaffold?" she asked. I could see concern showing in her eyes.

"The warehouse is quite big," I said. "All the work is over-head."

"Are you working on the scaffold?" she asked.

"Well, I have been, but we're almost done now."

"Why didn't you tell me before that you were working on a scaffold?" she demanded.

"Because I didn't want to worry you."

"How high in the air is it?" she probed.

"About thirty feet."

"Is it safe?"

"As safe as anything else, I suppose. The scaffold is a little shaky, but I'm careful."

"I had no idea that's what you were doing. I only wish you had told me earlier."

I could see fear growing in her eyes. I knew she would be worried. Now I wished that I hadn't told her until after I finished the job.

"Don't go to work tomorrow," she demanded.

"I can't do that. It's all been arranged. This is the only time I can hook up the compressor. Besides, there's no one to take my place. They're depending on me."

"But you can't go," she insisted.

"Why not?" I asked.

"I've had a terrible feeling for days," she said. "Now I know why. I'm afraid something's going to happen."

"That's nonsense," I retorted. "Nothings going to happen. If it was, it would have happened by now."

She persisted, now visibly shaken. "Please," she pleaded, "won't you stay home, for me? Can't you call in sick or something?" Then she became more insistent, "I don't want you to go in."

It was becoming a battle of wills. I was getting agitated at her insistence. "I have to go," I said. "I already told you I can't let them down. They're counting on me. Besides, you know I'm always careful. I haven't taken any chances on the scaffold yet, and I'm not about to start now. I always kneel down in the corner anytime anyone climbs up or down or when we move the scaffold. The scaffold is all set in one place now. We've already pulled the wire from the compressor to a junction box. The compressor end has already been hooked up. All I have to do now is pull the wire from the panel to the junction box and make the connections. Then we'll be done."

"I can't help it," she insisted. "I'm just so afraid something's going to happen."

With that we both fell into mute silence, drifting off into a restless sleep. The next morning, the 19th of September, 1972, as I prepared for work, Georgia persisted again.

"Are you sure you won't stay home?" she pleaded.

"No," I said firmly. "I've already told you why."

"Then please, promise me one thing?" she asked. "Promise me you won't go up on the scaffold today? Make someone else go up."

"I'll try," I said as I kissed her goodbye and headed down the road to work.

A New, Unknown Helper

When I reported to work, Reid, my boss, told me that my usual helper had called in sick and wouldn't be in.

"I can't do the job alone," I said. "I need some help to finish pulling in the wire."

"We've already called the warehouse and they said they'd let you use one of their people," Reid said.

I didn't want to complain or argue with him. Reid Knight was the kind of boss you wanted to impress. Opting out of a job was not the way to do it

I gathered what I needed and left. When I arrived, the warehouse supervisor had a man ready for me. We set about to complete all the preparations before noon. We laid out the wire, already cut to the proper dimensions by the supply house. After I was satisfied we were completely ready, we left for lunch early so we could be back and ready when the office staff left for lunch.

At 12:00 I shut the power off to the panel and sent my helper up on the scaffold as I shoved a fish tape through the conduit to him. He hooked a cable, which was attached to a hand crank, to the fish tape and fed it to me as I pulled it back to the panel. After I hooked the wire onto the cable, he began cranking the cable in on my signal. The wire went in smoothly until it hit the ninety-degree bend in the conduit at ceiling height. The wire stopped, unwilling to make the bend. One length of the wire had been replaced earlier by the supply house with a wire that was one size larger. Because of this, no matter how hard I shoved or my helper pulled, it wouldn't go around the bend.

I became frustrated and angry, knowing we were running out of time. I climbed the scaffold and tried to crank in the wire myself. Still, it wouldn't budge. I told my helper to go down and push from the other end. Although the wheels were locked in place, I still didn't trust the scaffold. I kneeled in the corner and held onto the life support line as I watched him climb down and start walking away.

The Scaffold Falls

Then it happened. With the sudden release of his weight the scaffold shifted, tottered, and began to fall as if pushed by a giant hand. Afterwards, eyewitness accounts to the accident told me that as the scaffold began to fall, I jumped up and grabbed the cross members of the ceiling. The way I was holding onto the cross beams, my knees were in line with the life line on the scaffold. It hooked me in the crook of the legs behind my knees when it started to fall over and I was unable to shake free. Because of the tremendous weight of the scaffold, I couldn't hold on.

Tremendous Physical Damage

As my grip on the cross members was ripped loose, my right shoulder was pulled from its socket and I was flung to the floor like a rock out of a sling shot.

Landing feet first, I fractured all the bones in both feet and drove the bones of my legs together, crushing my knees like eggshells and causing compound fractures above the left knee and to the inside of my right knee.

The muscles in my neck, chest and back, which give my right arm its lifting power, had also been torn loose when my arm was pulled from the socket.

After hitting the floor I fell to my knees, causing more damage to them. Then I pitched forward onto my right shoulder, permanently damaging the rotator cuff. I continued over, hitting my forehead on the concrete, which crushed in the frontal cavities of my forehead and peeled my scalp back.

My Heart Stops

A plumber who had been working just below me had narrowly missed being hit by the scaffold as it came down. Everyone working in the warehouse at the time came running when they heard me scream as I was thrown by the scaffold to the floor. They quickly made for the nearest exit when they saw me lying on the floor in the twisted scaffold with broken bones sticking out of my legs. I was a bloody, twisted mess. It made them all sick.

Only the plumber had the presence of mind to do anything. He jumped in and pulled me from the twisted scaffold. The trauma associated with the fall, together with the shock and pain from my injuries, caused my heart to stop. He immediately gave me mouth-to-mouth resuscitation and closed-heart massage until they could summon the paramedics. I was totally unaware of the revitalizing activities taking place.

Police and paramedics both quickly arrived on the scene and began first aid measures. Though I had no knowledge of what I was doing, I apparently revived and fought back against their efforts with superhuman strength. Three police officers and three paramedics pinned each of my arms down as they attempted to splint my legs. When they finished the splint on my left leg with the standard three ties, I bent my leg, which splintered the splints like so many match sticks. They doubled the splints this time and used six ties so I couldn't bend my leg again and cause more damage. After finishing with the splints, they began feverishly working on the rest of me in a desperate race with time, trying to save my life. The paramedic's devices were the only thing keeping my body alive.

For me, it was over. The fall had killed me.

Georgia's Account

Larry gave me a swift kiss and headed out the door. Our goodbye was quicker that morning than it normally was. Larry probably didn't want to give me another chance to try and convince him to stay home. In some things he was pretty headstrong, and he would refuse to listen to reason. I had tried to convince him last night of my premonition when I found he had been working on a scaffold.

For a week now I had been having a feeling that something was going to happen. I didn't say anything about my feelings because I couldn't find a reason for them. Nevertheless, last night when Larry told me that he had been working from a scaffold at work, I had a chilling feeling of dread. No matter what I said, it didn't seem to make a difference. I could see he was getting angry with me for insisting he stay home. I couldn't imagine what on earth could happen that would be as bad as the feeling I was getting.

I tossed and turned most of the night. What little sleep I did get was between taking care of the twins and worrying about Larry going to work the next day. It seemed every hour one or the other of the twins needed to be fed. When the twins were born, they told me at the hospital to keep a record when they were fed and who got fed last. I couldn't imagine not being able to remember which baby I had fed last. Now, after two-and-a-half months of being up almost all night, every night with the twins, I found they were right. I was having a hard time remembering which one I had fed last. Besides, they were sick. Even the faintest whimper would bring me to my feet to check on them. It was great moving into our first home. It had given us so much more room, and when we finished the basement off each one of the children could have their own room. But now I had to go further to tend the twins when they woke up and cried.

When I watched Larry drive off for work, all I could say was "Please, be careful." I tried to put my feelings behind me as I cleaned the house and took care of the kids. Nathan was a big help to me with Lori and the babies, but they were all so demanding of my time.

It was the middle of the afternoon when the phone rang. It was Reid's wife on the phone. She told me there had been an accident at work and they had taken Larry to the hospital. I almost became hysterical with concern wanting to know how he was and where they had taken him. She wanted to know if I had a car. I told her Larry had taken our only car to work that morning. Because of the panic in my voice she told me that he had only broken his leg.

She offered to pick me up and take me to the hospital. I wanted to know how soon she would be there. She said it would take her about twenty minutes. My mind raced after I hung up the phone. I was in a real panic because of the feelings I had been having—now they had come true. Larry was in the hospital with a broken leg. If only he had listened to me! I went next door and asked Mary Ann if she would watch the kids for me while I went to the hospital. She said, "Of course, I wouldn't mind." We went back to the house to prepare formula and make sure she had everything.

When Reid's wife pulled into the driveway, I ran to the car, slamming the door as I slid onto the front seat, scooting her young son over as I climbed in. As we pulled out and drove down the street I had a million questions I wanted answered. She said that they had taken Larry to the St. Marks hospital. It was the nearest hospital to where they had been working.

We were about half way to the hospital when her little boy blurted out, "But Mommy, I thought you said he had two broken legs!" She tried to hush him up but it was too late.

"What do you mean, two broken legs? I thought you only said he had one broken leg?"

"You just took it so hard when I told you he had gotten hurt—I didn't want to tell you he had two broken legs."

"What else is the matter with him?" I demanded.

"They only told us he had broken both of his legs and he was in pretty bad shape. I don't know anything more than what they told me on the phone."

"How did the accident happen?"

"He was on a scaffold and it fell over with him."

"I knew it. I knew something was going to happen. I could feel it." Sheer panic set in as I fought back the tears. "If only he had listened."

As we pulled into the entrance of the emergency room I was out and heading in the door before she had hardly brought the car to a stop. I told them who I was at the desk and wanted to know where Larry was. They asked me to wait a minute as they called the doctor.

As Dr. Smith introduced himself, he asked me to sit down and said he needed to talk to me first. "How serious could it be?" I demanded, wanting to know where Larry was and why I couldn't see him. Dr. Smith was trying to calm me down to prepare me for the worst.

"He has multiple compound fractures of both legs. He could have possible internal injuries; we're not sure yet. We're waiting for X-rays before we can do anything. He apparently hit his head when he fell. His face and head are bruised and swollen. He might have a concussion, we're not sure yet. Until we find the extent of his injuries, we can't give him anything for the pain. He's pretty busted up.

"There's no easy way to say this. There's a possibility he might not pull through this. If he does, I doubt he'll be able to walk again. Most likely he'll be in a wheelchair the rest of his life, if he makes it. You might want to call the family in. There's still time."

"Oh, my God!" I could hear myself saying. "This can't be happening. Please take me to him. I want to see him now."

"I just wanted to prepare you for what you're about to see."

"I don't care! Take me to him now."

Dr. Smith was grave as he gave me a Valium before leading me into the entrance of the examination room where Larry was. I could hear him now as he screamed out in pain and called for his mother over and over again.

I was not prepared in the least for what I saw. They had cut off Larry's pants. Even with splints on both legs, I could see part of the bones sticking out of his left leg. He was strapped down on the table, but even the straps didn't keep him from thrashing wildly about. His chest was black and blue. Blood was everywhere. His face was completely black and swollen. His eyes looked like small slits and were swollen completely shut. A large laceration on his forehead was peeled back, showing part of his skull.

Dr. Smith stood with his arms around me, supporting me so I wouldn't fall if I felt faint. I could only hold my hands to my mouth to try and hold back my choking sobs. He looked so bad. "You have to try everything," I sobbed to Dr. Smith as I turned to him. "You can't let him die."

He took me out of the examination room. "Are you going to be O.K.?"

"Yes," I cried. In my heart, though, I didn't know if I would be all right. When he left, I went to the phone. Mom and Dad said they would be right up when I talked to them. I asked if they would please call everyone for me.

I knew we were going to need all the help we could get so I called our bishop from our old ward, leaving a message imploring him to please come as fast as he could.

When I hung up the phone, I wasn't sure they would get my message so I called our new bishop. Bishop Boyer said they would be right up.

I called Mary Ann and told her what had happened, and asked her if she could take care of our babies until I came home. I knew she already had three rowdy boys of her own, but at the moment there wasn't anyone else I could turn to. She assured me they would be just fine, and told me not to worry about a thing.

All I could think of was what I was going to do if Larry died. All our glorious plans for the future were going right down the drain. If he died, we wouldn't be able to be married in the temple. How was I going to raise four little children by myself? Everything imaginable went through my mind.

I prayed to God to please not take him from me. I had finally found someone who loved me and was going to take care of me and the children. I prayed that I would be given the strength to make it through everything, praying stronger than I'd ever prayed in my life. Inside, feelings of hopelessness overwhelmed me.

The bishop and his two counselors from our old ward in Taylorsville had gotten my message. I was relieved to see them, but I couldn't stop the flood of tears. Between choking sobs I told them what had happened and asked if they would please administer to Larry. They assured me they would and then asked the nurse if it was all right if they went in. She said yes, but asked them to please not stay very long. I stood at the door watching as they approached him. Without any medication for his intense pain Larry began screaming out in pain, begging them not to touch him.

I couldn't imagine how much pain he was in but I knew we had no other choice. Minutes after they left, Bishop Boyer and his two counselors, the bishopric of our new ward, came into the emergency room where I was. I fell apart again as I told them what the doctor had said. They comforted me for a few minutes and then they went in to Larry. Again as I stood at the entrance I watched Larry as they approached him. As badly as his face was swollen, I didn't see how he could see anything but he still reacted like he did before. Afterwards, they assured me that they had done everything they could and it was in God's hands now. Bishop Boyer said he would organize the women in the ward to help with the children and give us all the assistance they could. I thanked him and slumped in my chair after they left, waiting for the doctor to make his determination.

It wasn't long before he came out and told me that they had developed the X-rays and they were preparing for surgery. Again he said they would do all they could.

Everyone was showing up now to help me wait out the long hours until he was out of danger.

5

My Entry into the Spirit World

I lay on my side after hitting the floor. I couldn't feel any pain. In fact, I couldn't feel anything. My first thought was, "Where is everyone?" I knew other people had been working in the warehouse but I couldn't see them.

I looked around. Several large overhead bay doors were opened and I could see the sunlight filtering through the haze. I also could see the foreman's office lined with glass windows and various support columns located throughout the warehouse.

I was confused as I began to lift off the floor and rose to an upright position. It was then I sensed I had died and was no longer inside my body. I was facing away from my body at the time and felt no desire to turn and look back at it.

The Foreboding Fog

As I looked about, everything had a light green cast, and I felt as though I were looking at everything through a light-green fog. It was the kind of a fog that seemed to pervade everything.

I was still feeling confused and bewildered as I began rising toward the ceiling. The closer I got to the ceiling, the thicker and darker the mist became, until at ceiling height it was as if I were standing in a very thick fog. It was as thick and foreboding as some of the worst fogs I've experienced while standing on the beaches in California, except this was far more mournful and desolate.

Agonized Souls in Outer Darkness

As I looked around, there seemed to be an endless sea of agonized souls floating in the fog. As some of them passed close by me, I could hear them moaning and groaning. The fog was so thick I could only make out their dim outlines. Their pain and grief washed over me. I was experiencing the uttermost feelings of the depths of despair. The overpowering feelings of frustration and misery I felt seeped into me with a cold that chilled my very soul. I was racked with terrible torment and anguish. The feelings were suffocating me.

"My God," I screamed. "Is this Hell? I can't stand it. Please God, help me." I pleaded with God to save me. I understood now what the scriptures mean when they talk about being cast out into outer darkness, and that the damned who are sent there moan and groan and thrash about and gnash their teeth because of their eternal despair.

A Loving Voice from the Light

I began ascending again and passed through the ceiling. Suddenly, a brilliant white light burst upon me. It was brighter than the sun and more intense. I was being pulled toward the light. I was drawn very close to it before I stopped.

As I stared intently into the light, I could faintly see facial features but nothing else. A soft, loving voice spoke to me from the light, and a peaceful calm came over me. I felt I was being comforted. I also felt an unconditional love directed to me.

Judging Myself in a Life Review

The being within the light uttered a phrase which I can't remember, but the phrase triggered a total recall of my life from the time when I was first born until the accident when I had died. My whole life passed before my eyes as if I were viewing a very vivid film. It was moving at a very high speed, and yet I could view each scene that unfolded with crystal clarity, and the speed seemed normal to me too.

It seemed as if I were judging myself, for I found no judgment from the being standing before me. Instead of condemnation, I felt an unconditional, loving tolerance such as a parent would feel toward his children after they'd done something wrong.

As the scenes of my life unfolded, I felt good knowing that I had handled certain situations very well. I could see how I had increased my spiritual development and advancement. But I didn't like other scenes I saw. I judged myself very harshly because of the way I had handled them. I thought to myself how much better I could have dealt with those situations. I found myself desperately wanting to go back to correct my actions in them. The things I had botched had retarded my spiritual development and had held me back. I was being much harder on myself than any judge could ever be.

Exhilaration as Earthly Impurities Are Stripped Away

As the last scenes of my life played to an end, I became aware that the light from the being had intensified considerably. I could feel my body changing. As I looked down, I could see the light burning through me with tremendous force. Earthly impurities were being stripped from me as large areas of my body were becoming transparent. I could see the outlines of my spiritual body filling these transparent areas. I experienced no pain as the impurities and imperfections were stripped away.

I felt a tremendous exhilaration and elation as the last of the impurities were stripped from me. Things which I had been burdened with on the earth were gone. I felt truly free. It was wonderful not to be plagued by my earthly imperfections any longer.

For the first time I really understood how much excess baggage we carry with us through this life and how things we struggle with and can't overcome while on the earth are burdens we carry with us all our lives. There are some burdens so great that we even carry them over with us into the spirit world.

The Importance of Forgiving Ourselves

I was told by the being that it was as important to forgive ourselves of our mistakes as it was to forgive others. The earth was a place for us to experiment and to learn. We would make mistakes along the way, but we would learn from our mistakes. Because we would make mistakes, it was important for us to learn to forgive ourselves.

I have learned that even God, the greatest of all, forgives us our sins and mistakes. Not being able to forgive ourselves only holds us back and keeps us from progressing. Our fear of personal failure is a quagmire which keeps us from trying anything.

A Parting View of Distant Earth

I felt whole, and complete, and more fully alive than at any time I can ever remember. When I turned and looked back at the earth, I was surprised to find it was so far away. I was seeing it from a great distance. It looked like a small, dirty brown ball, no bigger than a tennis ball. I felt a certain revulsion from the sight and was relieved and glad to be away from it.

Entry Through a Suspended Arched Doorway

I was directed to a doorway which seemed suspended in space. As I entered through it, I found myself standing in the middle of a room beyond the arched doorway. As I looked back, the same dark, green fog through which I had just passed was swirling and churning just beyond. The fog, which was so thick it looked almost black in color, was stopped at the doorway, unable to enter the room. It was repulsive and extremely distasteful to me and very unpleasant to look at. I felt as though I had just passed through Hell and never wanted to have to go through that fog again.

Clothed in White by Two Men

I found I had reentered the spirit world as I had the physical world, naked! Two men, both dressed in white robes, helped me put on a white, robe-like garment. As I adjusted the hem in the back, they left, disappearing into an office at the end of the hall.

The Names of Entrants Recorded in a Book

I looked up as I completed adjusting the hem on my robe. To the right of the doorway through which I had entered was a large desk. An old man with a long white beard wearing the same type of robe-like garment the others had worn was seated at the desk. He was writing in a large book. Without moving from my position I could see it was my name he was writing. I could also see the names of two other men he had recorded just before mine, and the name of a woman who apparently had entered before them. These were the names of people who had crossed over just before I had.

Several low benches of white crystallized marble were against one wall. Next to the doorway that entered onto the street was a low bench of a soft pink crystallized marble. The room itself appeared to be made of the same pink crystallized marble as the benches. Other than these, the room was void of any other furnishings. Everything was very soft and appealed to the senses.

Another door, closer in and to the left, was partially opened. The only thing I could see in the room was the corner of a desk and two pictures hanging on the wall. Another doorway, just opposite the one I had entered, opened onto a street.

Meeting Larry, My Assigned Guide

I suddenly realized a man was standing behind me and to my left, waiting for me to finish my robe adjustment. I turned as I became aware of him.

I almost didn't recognize him at first. Could I just be imagining it? I had to look again. I know this man, I thought. He had changed since I'd last seen him. Although his features were finer and his physical appearance more refined, I still recognized him as my friend, Larry Talbot, who had died.

I could hardly believe my eyes. I was so happy to see him! I threw my arms around him, hugging him. "Larry, Larry! I can't believe it's you. It's so good to see you. It has been so long. You have no idea how many times I've wanted to talk to you."

"Hello Larry," he said, exhibiting more restraint than I was. "I've been waiting for you. I've been assigned as your guide. I'm here to reinstruct you and to reeducate you until you are more familiar with your surroundings again."

Telepathic Speech

I realized that I hadn't seen his mouth move when he talked to me. It was like I was hearing him inside my head. "How can I hear you? I don't see you talking."

"It's a form of telepathy," he smiled. "It's one of the things you'll have to relearn. For your benefit you'll probably hear both ways for a while."

"Does everyone use telepathy here?" I asked.

"Everyone except the new ones like you who have just crossed over. If you're ready, we'd better get going. I have a lot to show you."

Greatly Increased Awareness as Former Knowledge Returns

As I followed Larry into the street, I was acutely aware of everything around me. "I've never felt like this before. I feel as if all my senses have increased a hundred fold," I said.

Larry smiled at me. "That's how I felt too when I first crossed over."

I felt I was again in possession of superior knowledge and intelligence that had been withheld from me since I had first gone to the earth.

"Yes," said Larry as if reading my thoughts. "Since you've crossed over, the veil has been taken from your mind. You'll soon regain all your powers and knowledge. It only takes a little time and the right words to jog your memory."

"It seems I've already had my memory jogged," I half-said to myself as I thought about the recall of my life I'd just been through.

"Ah yes," he said. "That was just a recall of your life. I'm talking about a recall of your former knowledge and powers."

"What powers are we talking about?" I asked.

"I'll try to explain as we go along," he said.

I looked around me. Everything was beginning to look familiar. "I feel like I've returned home," I said.

"You have," he assured me.

Description of the Street and Buildings

All the other buildings along the street consisted of the same soft crystallized material. Each reflected different colors of a soft, subtle nature. Because the street we stood on was so wide, I almost expected to see cars going up the street. Everything around me blended very harmoniously and was extremely pleasing to see. The buildings seemed to be part of a small town square. The community wasn't large at all. The center only consisted of about four city blocks, and the town was only several blocks wide. Most of the buildings were only about four stories tall. A few were one-story structures. The rest were two-story buildings.

A Glimpse of the Glory of God

At one point, as we crossed the street, I looked as far down the street as I could. I could see a brilliant golden white light, almost like the sun. When I looked at it, I expected to feel pain in my eyes like I've felt before when I looked at the sun.

To my amazement there wasn't any. Instead, I felt a great love coming from the light. Beautiful golden rays radiated in every direction. Every object seemed to glow as it reflected the rays of this golden light. I stood, staring in awe at the light. It was the most beautiful thing I had ever seen.

I could feel an all-encompassing love as the golden rays enveloped me. I felt secure and more loved at that moment than I can ever remember. The words "brotherly love" took on a whole new meaning as I began to more-fully comprehend the unity of God's creations. I sensed in this grand design that we're all linked with each other through this love, as literal brothers and sisters—children of our Heavenly Father. I also felt a kinship with the universe through this universal spirituality and intelligence we shared. I closed my eyes, basking in this love light, relishing the warm, vibrant feelings that flooded through me.

"What you are seeing," said Larry softly, "is the Glory of God."

"The source of the light is God," said Larry. "His glory shines to the ends of his creations. All the laws of the universe and the love of his creations glorify him and sing praises to him and give thanks for their existence. The greatest of all his creations are his children. They are the greatest recipients of his love."

Musical Ecstasy

As I opened my eyes and looked at the light again, I could faintly hear music, and yet I could feel the music vibrating through me too. It was a haunting, melodic, musical symphony. Now that I was aware of the music, I could feel and hear it coming from everything around me, from every direction and from every object. I felt on the verge of tears with the sheer ecstasy I was experiencing. How beautifully the sounds blended together!

Everyone Attends His Own Funeral

We began moving slowly down the street again. The buildings were becoming more familiar. My chest heaved with emotions as I turned to Larry. "We have so much to talk about. I've missed you so much. I'm just so glad it was you that met me. You have no idea how often I wished I could have seen you, just once."

"I was at the funeral," said Larry. "Only you couldn't see me. I liked very much the things you said about me."

Shocked, I turned to him. "You were there?" I asked.

"Oh yes! Only no one knew it. Everyone attends their own funeral. I guess you could say we get the chance to officiate at them."

"How come we go to our own funeral?" I asked.

"It's necessary," he said. "There are those we've left behind that need comforting. Besides, there will come a time when we'll need to know where our bodies are."

"But why is that?" I asked.

"When the resurrection comes we'll be reunited with our bodies as we become resurrected beings. It's a necessary part of our progression."

"Will I be attending my own funeral also?" I asked. The thought of seeing myself, or at least my body being buried didn't appeal to me.

"Yes, you will. After a short recuperation period such as you're going through now."

The Council Chambers

Stopping, Larry asked as he gestured with his hand, "Do you know where we are?"

I looked at the buildings around us. We were standing in front of a building that housed the council chambers. I smiled at the recognition. Forgotten memories of meetings I used to attend were starting to surface. "Yes," I said. "These are the council chambers. I thought things looked familiar."

The Decision: Stay or Return

Larry paused. "I've brought you here for a reason. You see, you're not dead yet. That is, your body is still being kept alive on earth. A final decision hasn't been made yet. This will depend on you. The council's meeting inside now. There is still a chance you could go back."

"Go back!" I was stunned. "I didn't think I could, not after coming this far."

The implications began to sink in. What had I left behind? Did I really want to go back? I thought about Georgia and the kids. Would I be cheating them if I stayed? It would be so easy to stay, but I loved Georgia. It had taken so long to find her, and now I was about to lose her again! I remember I had made sacred promises to her that I would take her through the temple. Now if I stayed I would lose my chance. And the kids. What about all my promises to them? Now I knew that if there was a chance to return, I had to go for it. I had to go back.

You're Here Before Your Time

"Do you think it could be possible to go back, Larry?" I asked.

"You had a lot of years left. What happened to you was an accident. You're here before your time. You could decide to stay here. If you do your body will cease to function. The only reason you still have a chance to go back is that your body can still sustain life. The choice now is yours."

As Larry had said, the council was in session. I knew what I had to do. Somehow, I had to convince them to reconsider and send me back. I had to try.

"I have to go in, Larry. Will you wait for me?"

"I was hoping you would," he said, smiling.

6

The Council

The Council Chambers

The building we were standing in front of gave the impression of being a two-story building. Actually it was only one-story tall, even though it was taller than the other single-story buildings.

Five granite steps led up from the street to two massive, dark-brown doors. Somehow they seemed out of place. It was as if they distinctively set the building apart from the others.

As I stood before the familiar doors and knocked, a voice from inside said, "Yes? Come in."

I cautiously opened the door and stepped inside. The room had remained much the same since I was last there. The same large table occupied the center of the room. Book shelves stood against one wall. Opposite me, across the table, were a number of chairs where most of the council members were seated. I was impressed by the stillness in the room. All eyes were on me.

Presenting My Request to the Council

The council appeared to be patterned after other groups I'd seen when I attended church meetings back on earth. The person in charge was flanked by two other council members who assisted him. The rest of the council was made up of nine other members, making twelve in all.

The one in charge was standing, addressing the group, when I entered. "Yes? Can we help you?" he asked.

I stepped forward hesitantly. "May I have permission to address the council?"

He looked at me. "You're Larry, aren't you?"

"Yes I am," I answered.

He smiled as he sat down. "Yes you may," he said.

I stepped to the table and looked at the group. "It's been some time since I was here last," I said. "I've been on earth and have just crossed over. I'm here by mistake. I'm not supposed to be here yet. I would like you to reconsider and send me back."

"Why do you say mistake?" they asked.

"I'm only here because of an accident. I feel it wasn't my time to die yet."

Many Enter by Mistake and Are Sent Back

"Then why were you not stopped and sent back before this?" the leader asked, rising to his feet. "Many people do enter here by mistake and are sent back, but always before they get this far."

"I don't know. I think maybe because I'm not supposed to go back. I'm not sure, though. I've been told that my body is being kept alive. This is why I think I'm here by mistake."

My Reasons for Wanting to Return

"What reasons have you for wanting to go back?" he asked.

I nervously looked at the group of men patiently waiting to hear my reasons. This would be my only chance. Somehow, I had to convince them. I quickly collected my thoughts as I mustered my courage. Memories of Georgia had slowly begun to return. Memories of our pre-mortal life and of the promises I had made were becoming more focused as I began speaking.

"The one I love so very much," I began, "was born shortly after I was. We had been together here for millennias of time before being sent to the earth. I had made certain promises to her—that after we had arrived on the earth, I would find her and take her through the temple. It's taken me almost thirty years to find her. We have just recently gotten married in a civil ceremony and have completed all the preparations for going through the temple. We were only waiting for permission and then we were going to go through.

"We have four small children, two of them just tiny babies. You see, we had all made certain agreements here before being born that we won't be able to keep unless I can go back. I'm only here now because of the accident. I know my time's not up yet. This is why they are still able to keep my body alive.

"You see, you've just got to let me go back. I have to fulfill my promises. I want to be able to take my love through the temple personally and to be sealed to her. Without me, we'll lose the children. I know they won't have the opportunities that only I can give them. No one else will be able to give them the love I can.

"We have just moved into our first home. Georgia won't be able to keep it if I'm not there. It'll cause the whole family to break up. I really feel I'm needed there more than I'm needed here."

I was becoming more emphatic as I emphasized each point. I was getting carried away and I was beginning to repeat myself.

"You've just got to let me go back!" I demanded, pounding my fist on the corner of the desk. "You've just got to let me go back!"

I suddenly realized what I was doing and stopped. I realized the council had been very patient with me by allowing me to express myself in such a manner.

The Implications of Returning: Pain and Temptations

"Are you prepared to go back?" asked the leader. "Do you have any idea what you'll be going through if you go back?"

"I believe I do," I said.

He looked me squarely in the eye, as if to impress upon me the gravity of my request and the implications it involved as he spoke.

"You'll be going back to a body that's badly broken and smashed. You'll experience unbelievable pain in the months to come, just for you to recuperate. Back on earth you'll still be subject to all the temptations of the flesh. There is no guarantee that you'll be able to keep your promises. With your children's free agency, you could still lose them. We will not interfere with theirs nor with your free agency. I have only scratched the surface of what you'll be faced with. Are you prepared for all that?"

"Yes I am," I said resolutely. "At least, I'd like to try. My family will stand a better chance if I'm there."

I knew that to say anything else would be futile. Whatever their decision, I would have to abide by it.

The Council Agrees to Consider My Request

"We shall have to discuss your request. We will inform you as to our decision," he said, dismissing me.

"Thank you," I said, bowing my head and backing out the door. I hoped I hadn't diminished my chances by being so emphatic.

7

Genealogical and Temple Work

Flying Through the Air as We Begin Our Tour

Larry was waiting patiently for me when I rejoined him in the street.

"They have to think about it for a while. They'll contact me later when they make a decision," I told him.

"Well, then. Let's finish our tour," he said. "There is so much I want to show you. Besides, I have a surprise for you later on."

I didn't question him, I only allowed myself to be led. Larry took me by the hand as we rose into the air, moving off toward a large grove of trees in the distance.

The Genealogical Research Center

A beautiful white-domed building lay sprawled among the trees. We gently alighted on the front steps. From the air the building hadn't appeared to be very large. From inside it looked immense. The ceilings were much higher than they needed to be. The building was designed to be very light and airy, with large expansive windows allowing the light to penetrate to every nook and cranny. The section we entered was connected by a long hall to other parts of the building. The outside section of the hall had high windows flanked by white-ribbed marble columns that arched to the ceiling.

The inside wall was continually lined with doors which opened into large rooms containing shelf after shelf of books and manuscripts. Comfortable-looking chairs and tables were interspersed among the columns of books.

We had crossed to the other end of the building. The hall opened into a very large, circular room. Here again, as in the hall, tall windows rose toward the ceiling, stopping where the domed ceiling started. An ornately sculptured section completely circled the room, separating the dome from the walls. Narrow triangular windows arched up toward the center of the dome above this separation, and between the continuations of the columns that separated the windows in the walls. The columns, the windows in the dome, and the walls aligned perfectly. They were broken in their continuation only by the ornately designed section between the dome and the walls.

Low shelves filled with books and papers were distributed throughout the room. Large numbers of people were busying themselves looking through different books and carrying papers back and forth. Because of the size of the room, it appeared to be almost vacant despite the large number of people present.

Once inside, I remarked to Larry what a beautiful library I thought it was.

"This is not a library," he said, chuckling. "This is one of our research centers. Here, interested people are busy gathering records and tracing their genealogical lines."

"Why do they need to do that?" I asked. "I thought that was something people just did on earth."

"Oh no," said Larry. "These records are very important. Without them their ordinances cannot be performed for them here."

"But I thought once they had the records and the ordinances were done on the earth, that was all that needed to be done."

Ordinances Performed Vicariously on Earth Also Are Performed by Recipients in the Spirit World

Larry thought for a moment and then said, "Haven't you heard the expression, 'as it is on earth, so shall it be in heaven'?"

"Well yes. But what does that have to do with it?"

"O.K. then. It's no different here. Having performed one's ordinances on the earth is only half of it. Those same ordinances must be performed here to be complete.

"When people have their work done for them by someone else on the earth, they're under no obligation to accept it. If they do accept the work done in their behalf, then those same ordinances and work must be performed here, by them, to be binding.

"Everything on the earth and in heaven goes hand in hand. Everything that exists on the earth was created in heaven first. Likewise, whatsoever shall be sealed on the earth shall be sealed in heaven, and whatsoever is loosed in heaven shall be loosed on the earth."

Spirit World Research Often Revealed to Those on Earth

Larry let me ponder on the things he had just said before he continued. "Genealogical research is progressing very rapidly on the earth, but because of the history of the earth, many records are lost, incomplete, or impossible to find. Broken family lines can be bridged by the research that's done here. Family members here often have handed completed family records and genealogical research over to someone on the earth who is doing the research for that family."

"Yes, I understand what you're saying. I never realized how important it was," I said. "I can see why someone would want the work done. I guess I just don't understand why we need to be sealed as complete family lines though."

"No, you don't understand," said Larry. He thought for a minute and then continued. "You think genealogical research is just gathering the names of your ancestors so their ordinance work can be done and that's all."

"Well that," I added, "and to try and trace our family ties back to Adam and Eve."

"There's more to it than that," said Larry. "Let me explain it to you this way." As he began speaking, a clear image appeared in my mind, detailing what he was saying in a way that no spoken words could ever do.

Vivid Mental Imagery: Golden Links

Pure golden links the color of translucent amber, that radiated with a golden glow of their own, appeared in my mind. Certain golden links were single and hung in the air at a certain level. Some of these were a little higher or lower than the others, but were all about the same level. Other golden links were joined in groups of twos or threes.

There were several groups of the golden links joined to form long chains. Single links weren't as high nor shone as brilliantly as those that were linked together. The more links that were joined, the higher in the air they were and the brighter they shone. The long golden chains were very high, and their combined light made the sun pale in comparison.

Larry explained, "All of Father's children are important in his sight. He has stated that his work and glory is to bring to pass the immortality and eternal life of man. In other words, his children.

"Each person is a pure golden link possessing certain powers and glory. Each is limited in the power or glory he possesses. Genealogical research provides all the required information so that as their ordinances are performed, they are joined to or sealed to other family members or ancestors. As they become sealed, their combined powers increase, as does their glory, allowing them to rise closer to the glory or perfection of God the Father."

Partaking of the Powers and Glory of Eternal Life

Larry continued, "Long family lines that have been sealed together contain immense power. That power is reflected by the glory that radiates from them. These groups are close to the highest realm in God's kingdom—in other words, the celestial kingdom. In this way, his goals are accomplished. As all mankind becomes sealed through their genealogical research work, their powers combine and their glories increase, approaching the glory of the Father himself.

"Because of this, we will one day become one with Father as we become like him, sharing the greatest gift he has ever given his children. We'll share immortality and eternal life and possess the same degrees of power and glory that he does."

I was so taken up by the visions of his explanations that I forgot for a moment where I was. "I never realized how important it was before this. Now I understand the significance that's placed on genealogy. It was never explained like that to me before," I said.

"Simple explanations are like the tip of the iceberg," explained Larry. "The whole picture or depth of the iceberg too often is hidden from view. It's just like simple explanations. They don't bring to light the full impact and understanding of the deeper gospel principles they embody."

"I feel the implications of what you've explained to me are enormous, yet so simple. I feel as if the entire gospel plan is founded on this one simple principle," I said.

"Now the memory of your pre-existence is coming back," said Larry. "When you remember everything, then you'll understand all of Father's gospel doctrines. You are just now starting to remember, which, like I said, is just the tip of the iceberg."

"We need to be going," said Larry. "I know you'd like to see more here at the center, but I have so much more I want to show you before we run out of time."

"Run out of time?" I asked. "That's funny. I thought we had all the time in the world."

"We would," Larry said, "if you were staying."

"Oh yes. I see what you mean. What else do you want to show me?" I asked.

8

Learning Centers and Absorbing Knowledge

The Flying Experience Again

I followed Larry through the research center. Once outside, he took me by the hand as we lifted off the ground.

"I want to show you some of our learning centers," Larry said. I could see he was amused at my wonderment.

"This is really a terrific way to travel," I said. "But why do you always take my hand when we fly like this?"

"This is something you'll need to relearn," he said. "It's easier if I just include you for now. Later, you'll be able to do it for yourself."

A Learning Center

I could see several groups of people ahead as we approached. We came to a stop in the air about twenty feet from a group. The group was divided by a partition in the form of a cross or an `X' so as to form four separate classroom groups. There were no walls nor ceilings except for the partition.

"This is just one of the many learning centers we have here," said Larry.

Below, I could see a class studying as they were taking periodic notes. One of the other classes was doing painting and sculpting. A third group was involved with a lecture. We dropped down to the ground before I could tell what the last group was doing.

We walked among the group that was studying. They paid no attention to us. Occasionally I would stop to look over someone's shoulder.

Great Joy in the Pursuit of Knowledge

"What are they studying?" I asked.

"Just about everything," he said. "It isn't important what you study. This isn't like it is on earth. Here, everyone has a burning thirst for knowledge. One of our greatest joys here is the pursuit of knowledge."

"Somehow, I thought it would be different. I don't know what I thought heaven was going to be like," I said. "It certainly wasn't this."

"You'll find we don't learn the traditional way either," he said. "We have many different methods of learning. Remember what I said about the tip of the iceberg. There's much more to all this than what you're seeing.

Advanced Ways of Learning: Absorbing Knowledge

"Take, for example, that man over there," said Larry, gesturing to the man closest to us. "What you see is him reading a book. Actually, he's reading for pleasure. If he wanted to learn about the book he could simply hold it. He would absorb the entire contents of the book and never have to open its cover. If he so desires he would also be able to comprehend everything about the book: the chemical composition of the book, how it was made, the methods of printing, everything. He would be able to discern what the author had in mind when he wrote the book and be able to experience every feeling and emotion the author felt as he wrote the book.

"This is true of most everything here. We're able to absorb knowledge by holding or simply touching, seeing, being close to something or by being part of a group such as this. Many things are transmitted telepathically. We in essence absorb knowledge through every part of our bodies. Knowledge itself is useless without the experience to go with it," Larry continued.

Knowledge Increases Our Intelligence

"What do you mean by experience?" I asked.

I followed Larry to the other side of the partition.

"Now, these people are learning by experience. They've studied sculpting and painting from books, classroom study, visiting other sculptors, and by holding objects. Then they do on their own from what they've learned. Like everything else, we get better the more we do it. Perfection takes time."

"Not everyone is good at the same things though," I said.

"That's true," said Larry. "That is because we have different talents and interests. As we get better at what we're doing, that is, building on or perfecting our talents, we're given other talents. Our knowledge and interests are expanding all the time.

"The one thing we've all learned is that knowledge increases our intelligence. The greater our field of knowledge and experience, the more intelligent we become."

"One thing's for sure," I said. "We've got a lot to learn. Just look at all of Father's creations. If we're going to be like him we have an awful lot to learn."

"Now you know why we have our burning passion for knowledge. If we're going to inherit Father's Kingdom, we need to be intelligent enough to administer in the affairs of the Kingdom."

9

Powers and Abilities

A thirst for knowledge. Yes, that's what it seemed like. As I thought back over my life, it did seem as though I'd always been curious about everything. I wasn't always satisfied with taking something apart to see how it worked. I also wanted to know *why* it worked. More curiously, I wondered what thought process led up to the creation of the object.

Projecting and Protecting Our Thoughts Through Telepathy

"What are you thinking?" asked Larry.

What was I thinking? I looked at him, wondering if he could read my thoughts "Do you know what I'm thinking?" I asked.

He didn't reply, only looked at me. I felt I needed to clarify myself. "I mean, if you can speak telepathically, then can you read my thoughts?"

"Actually, no I can't. It's a rather difficult process to explain. It's true we can send and receive thoughts. When you relearn the process, you'll understand more fully. For now let me just say that your thoughts are private. If you need to communicate with someone, then you project out to that person. You can think out to someone, or to a whole group, or to everyone here. When you're only thinking to yourself, your mind has a way of shutting out or shielding itself from thought leakage. In this way your privacy is protected."

"This could be very useful on earth," I said, half jokingly. "It would save a lot on phone bills." Larry smiled at my little joke, which made me feel better.

"Telepathy is the purest form of communication," he said. "There could not possibly be any misunderstanding this way. If I were to send you a message telepathically, you'd see it exactly as I saw it, as I sent it. For instance, if I told you that I wanted to meet you in the park, you'd want to know what park, where in the park, an exact location. I would use words to describe everything the way I understood them. You might not have the same definition for the words I chose. Therefore, a misunderstanding. But, if I sent a message telepathically to you of the same park, you'd see the exact spot as well as the park I had chosen. Therefore, you wouldn't misunderstand because of the different definitions for the words we use."

I thought about that for a moment as his words soaked in. "You mean like when you were describing genealogy to me?"

"Exactly," said Larry.

"That's powerful," I said. "It was like I was experiencing it at the same time."

"That's why it's the purest form of communication," Larry said. "You not only see what I see, you also experience the emotions I feel at the time. Therefore, it's as if you're actually experiencing the message yourself. It can get to be quite emotional, especially if you're not used to it."

"Earlier you said you would explain to me about the powers and abilities we would possess. Is telepathy one of them?" I asked.

Levitation a Power of Spirit Intelligence

"Yes it is," answered Larry.

"I guess that flying is one of them also?" I asked.

"Yes," he said. "Except it's not actually flying. I know that's what it appears to be but it isn't. In one sense it's a form of levitation. What we are is spirit intelligence. We are governed by a different set of divine laws and principles than are all the other creations in Father's Kingdom. So in that sense we're not affected in the same way nor by the same laws."

"Is that why we're able to move through and even stand in the air without falling?" I asked.

"That's right. It takes getting used to. It won't take long before you'll feel completely at ease with it. It'll just become a natural way of doing things."

"Somehow I feel like we're talking about the tip of the iceberg again. It seems more than I can comprehend right now," I said.

"I know it's difficult for you now. You just haven't shaken off the shackles of earth life yet. It's very difficult for some to comprehend these celestial principles.

"We all progress at our own rate here. I'm giving you more than you can understand in the short time we have."

Some Principles
Don't Apply to People on Earth

"Yeah, it's hard to understand, and yet I've got an open mind. I'm quicker to believe and accept what you're telling me than a lot of people I know would be.

"How would you explain these things to someone who hasn't been over here yet? Some people can't even understand simple principles, let alone what you're telling me," I said in exasperation.

"We can't," said Larry. "The ideas and principles that I've been describing don't usually apply to people on the earth. Remember, their memories have been taken from them. They're living by earthly principles and precepts. In their restricted thinking they can barely understand the simpler precepts, let alone the things I've shown you."

"If I get to go back, will I be able to remember what I've seen?" I asked.

"Yes, it's possible," said Larry. "What you have to under-stand is that you've been through a very traumatic experience. Sometimes in order to protect itself, the brain will block out the extremely traumatic experiences. This can happen because the shock of what has happened is greater than the brain can with-stand. Other times there is such great pain involved that the brain will completely block it out. When this happens, the per-son involved will generally experience amnesia and won't be able to remember anything that has happened.

"Also, if you go back, the veil will probably drop across your mind again. If that happens, then you probably won't remember anything. Besides, there are things here that you're not supposed to know. These things will be blocked from you for your own good. Otherwise, your free agency would be taken away. Your capacity to experience and learn, and thereby your progression, would be taken away."

I thought of what Larry had said. A great trauma could block out our memories. Is this why babies can't remember their pre-mortal life—because of the trauma of being born? I remembered reading several accounts of very young children talking about places they've been and people they'd seen just before they were born. They had been shown pictures of people that had already died before they were born, and yet they had been able to remember them.

The impact of what I'd been through and seen here had been too great for me not to be able to remember. And yet, I hadn't been able to remember anything of my pre-existence before crossing over. Maybe, just maybe, I would be able to remember.

The Circumstances of Larry's Death

I studied Larry as I thought things over. There was so much to grasp. And still I had questions about our relationship that I never found the answers to.

"Could I ask you some personal questions?" I asked.

Larry looked at me as if pondering my question. "Sure. Go ahead."

"I've always wondered exactly what happened . . . ," I faltered, searching for the correct words. "I mean, well, I mean . . . , what happened when you died?" Now I wished I hadn't asked. I felt uncomfortable, as if I were prying into something that wasn't any of my business. "I'm sorry," I said, trying to think of something else to say.

"It's O.K." said Larry. "I don't mind talking to you about it." He paused for a minute, collecting his thoughts. "We've seen enough here," he said. "Let's go. There's still more for you to see."

10

A Kingdom Governed by Beauty and Order

L arry again took me by the hand and we rose, moving away, crossing some low, tree-lined hills. It wasn't long before we settled onto a well-groomed street where large trees that looked like huge oaks lined the street on either side. As we walked side by side down the street, Larry began talking to me.

"What happened to me," said Larry, "was the result of my foolish actions. I hadn't anticipated the consequences of what I was doing."

"I was told it was accidental," I said. "I put the pieces together and concluded that you must have bumped your head, knocking yourself unconscious."

"That's right. That's just what happened," he said. "After you left me that morning, I tried to stretch myself again. The chair I used to stand on had a short leg that made it rock slightly. After I slipped the noose under my chin, the chair rocked because of that short leg, startling me. I over-reacted, and that caused the chair to flip out from under me. I fell backwards, hitting my head against the door. It knocked me out. When I bounced forward the noose slipped over my head. It was too late to do anything. In a few moments I was dead."

Everyone Entering the Spirit World Is Escorted by a Guide

I stopped and looked at Larry. "What was it like?" I asked. "When I heard what had happened, I couldn't believe it. I took it pretty hard." This was all still so new to me. I was looking for some kind of comparison to my own experience.

"Did you go through the same thing I did when you died?" I asked.

"Yes I did," he said. "After I died, I just looked at my body for a long time. I felt remorseful at first. I didn't know how to handle it. When I was finally admitted into the receiving room where I met you, I was taken on a tour just like the one I'm taking you on."

"Were you met by someone you knew too?" I asked.

"Yes," he said. "Everyone is. It makes the transition easier that way."

I didn't ask who his guide was. I felt I would be prying into an area that would be too personal. I grappled with my feelings. There were so many unanswered questions. I needed time to sort through my emotions and digest what was happening to me.

"This situation shouldn't be this hard to understand, should it?" I asked.

Larry sensed what I was feeling. "It isn't, only at first. When your memory completely returns you'll be able to understand it all. You'll see the perfect logic and harmony in all this."

Spirit-world Homes Built as a Result of Earthly Deeds

"Come on," Larry said. "Let's continue." As we moved around some bushes by the sidewalk, Larry called my attention to a beautiful, white, two-story home. A beautiful, middle-aged woman was grooming some flowering plants that were growing at the end of the house. A spacious green lawn completely encompassed the house, disappearing into the trees behind.

"Whose house is this?" I asked.

"It belongs to that lady there," he said.

"She lives here? This is her home?" I asked in amazement.

"Yes," Larry said. "This is the mansion she built for herself while she lived on the earth."

I could feel the peace and serenity she surrounded herself with. "Does everyone live like this?" I asked, trying to judge the size and depth of the mansion before me.

Acts Performed on Earth Recorded in the Spirit World

"Everyone could, if they lived their lives according to the gospel of Jesus. This woman has earned her rest here through her unselfish service to others. She spent her whole life helping everyone she came in contact with. In the eyes of the world she went largely unnoticed. Only here were the deeds recorded as she performed each unselfish task. By her deeds, she built her mansion, one piece at a time.

"Her last earthly act was in service to her family. She gave her life so that her youngest child could live. Her love was unconditional as she followed the example set down by Jesus. No greater love hath a man than he lay down his life for another. As he lay it down, so shall he take it up again in glory as he resides in the Kingdom of Heaven."

The woman looked up at us and smiled as she carried flowers into her home.

Helping Others the Greatest Work We Can Do on Earth

"You see," said Larry, "the greatest work we can do while on the earth is to help others. By giving of your time and your abilities, you won't have time to think or worry about your own problems. The real joy comes from the peace and fulfillment we gain through our service to others. Besides, this gives others the opportunity to help us in return.

"This is so beautiful. Could I live in a house like this?" I asked, almost to myself.

"I can't tell you that yet," he said. "Only after we know whether you're going back or staying."

Father's Kingdom Governed by Beauty and Order

As we moved on down the street, I saw homes that boggled my imagination. As we approached from the air, I could see a very large number of homes. Beautifully manicured yards lined the streets. Each house was set in among large, spreading trees. Now, as we walked down the sidewalk in front of the houses, it was like each house was completely by itself. It was almost as if the house next to it didn't exist. Each person's privacy seemed assured. Looking past the houses we passed, I could see into the distance behind them. Trees appeared to go on forever, yet from the air we could see that other homes were right behind them.

This was another of the paradoxes I was experiencing since I crossed over. On one level things appeared to be a normal size, but on the other they seemed immense.

This paradox was just like the genealogical center we had just been to. From the outside it appeared to be just a normal-sized building, but from the inside it was immense. The review of my life had been the same way. I viewed everything at a high speed, yet every scene was acted out at a normal pace.

Also, there was the town square Larry had taken me through when we left the receiving area. I had the impression that it was an immense city, yet it only covered about a four-block area.

Here again, I was in a residential area that from the air seemed well defined and laid out. Even though the homes were spaced evenly, each appeared to be completely isolated and alone. The area around each home offered it complete privacy and made it feel like it was sitting in the middle of a forty-acre field.

"Is everything like this?" I asked, looking around in amazement. "Nothing seems out of order. There are no weeds, trash or garbage of any kind anywhere."

"Father's Kingdom is governed by beauty and order," he said. "This is not like it is on earth. Harmony and beauty are built into every creation here.

"Man brings discord and turmoil into his life because he pulls away from Father's teachings. If men on the earth lived their lives as Father had designed, then heaven and earth would actually become one, with no separation between them. The veil between would disappear."

All Matter Exists at Certain Vibrational Frequencies

"If people could see this as I'm seeing it, they'd understand. I'm sure they'd live their lives differently," I stated.

"If men lived their lives right, then they would be able to elevate themselves spiritually and be able to see," said Larry.

"I'm not sure I understand," I said.

"All matter exists at certain vibrational frequencies. Spiritual or heavenly things vibrate at a higher frequency than do earthly things. This is why the spiritual or heavenly things are almost invisible to those on the earth.

"So it is with good and evil. The more man turns from God's way and embraces evil, the more coarse he becomes. He actually vibrates at a lower frequency, thereby widening the gap between himself and God.

"On the other hand, the more spiritual a man becomes and the more he embraces Father's teachings, the higher his vibrational frequency becomes. Men can become so spiritual that their vibrational frequencies can become concordantly harmonious. A convergent frequency is born between heaven and earth, and there is no separation between the two places."

"That's deep," I said. "You really got me on that one. So much for simple explanations."

Larry laughed. "We will get into this more later on," he said. "Just believe me for now. There's a purpose for everything under heaven and earth."

A Different Description of Hell

"I can't imagine what other places are like for those who haven't lived like they should," I said.

"You'd be very sorrowful for them. You'd see the hell they're going through," he said.

"Is it anything like the hell I passed through right after I died?" I asked.

"No, not that bad," he said. "Just imagine being cut off from Father's light. Living in darkness, away from his light, is pure hell for some. Always being able to see the best but not being able to have it also is hell.

"This is why progression is so important. It allows us all the opportunity to accept and believe and be part of the light. This is the mercy of a just Father. He wants us all to learn and accept his light and to eventually become one with him."

"This really is the best, isn't it?" I asked, looking about me at the regal splendor before me.

"Come with me," he said. "I'll show you the best that heaven has to offer."

11

The Celestial City

Approaching the Boundary of God's Celestial Kingdom

The countryside beneath us fell quickly away as Larry and I rose higher and higher. A pale luminescence ahead held my attention as we approached. The light became increasingly more brilliant as the distance decreased. I struggled to visualize the shapes that began to form. We still were a long way from the source of the light as Larry and I stopped on a sloping hillside.

A Celestial City Viewed from Afar

"We can go no farther," he said. "Just ahead lie the bounds of our travel."

The hillside ahead continued its ascent, ending at the base of a mountain. Cliffs rose steeply, disappearing into a hazy mist. Very high mountains protruded through the mist as fleecy clouds slowly drifted across their craggy peaks. Regal splendor crowned this celestial scene.

At the base of the mountains lay a glorious city. Tall spires and pinnacles rose in exalted splendor, challenging the clouds above for dominance.

Light radiated, undulating from the pearlized buildings. A thousand different shades of color filled the spectrum. I struggled to comprehend the sheer immensity of the city that lay before me. At first, I failed to see the delicate details of the domed spires until I studied the scene in more detail.

Each spire's dome was capped in pure gold. Pinnacles the color of platinum rose among the spires.

My emotions overcame me as I sank to my knees in the tall grass at my feet. Through each arched doorway and window shimmered a faint blue light.

Restricted to Those Who Have Attained Celestial Status

"This," said Larry, "is the best."

"What is this?" I asked in utter amazement.

"This is the Celestial Kingdom. From here, Father directs all the affairs of his creations. Only those very special spirits that have obtained celestial status may reside there.

"For all the rest of us, we may only be content to view it from a distance. It is out of bounds and out of reach for us. Eventual perfection will afford us passage within, but until then we must be content to inhabit the lower Kingdoms."

Feeling the City's Divinity

"I can feel the utter divinity of the city," I breathed through a hushed breath. "I can't understand the feelings I feel. I've never felt anything like this before. Even after all you've shown me, I still haven't had feelings like this. I can't explain it."

More memories came flooding back as I recalled an earlier time. It was a time when we were all part of God's celestial world. It was a time in which we all participated in the preparations for our mortal existence on the earth. Most of us remained true and faithful to Father, thus earning the right to come to the earth and take a body. We had gained the right then to leave our celestial home so that we might be tried and tested on the earth.

For most, being able to see what we were once part of and not being able to obtain it again or to look at what we once had as I was doing now, would be a very real hell in itself. Knowing the very real possibility existed that we might never regain it was very overwhelming to me.

"You don't have to try to explain it," said Larry. "I've felt the same thing every time I come here. I can't find the words to express what I feel either."

"Of all Father's creations, none can match the magnificence of his Celestial Kingdom," he added.

Father Protects Our Heavenly Mother

I hardly dared utter what I was thinking. "Is this God's home?" I asked.

"Yes," answered Larry.

"Then if this is his home, is this our Mother's home also?" I queried. "I've often wondered about her, but never really knew for sure if we really did have a mother here," I said. "I wonder why we've never heard more about her."

"Yes, this is her home also. Father knows the limits of our mortal understanding and comprehension. He recognizes that his name is sometimes profaned and trampled upon by his children. They sometimes exploit and trample underfoot all that he has given them.

"He loves and cherishes her above all else. He won't allow her name to be had by the mortal children of his creation so they can't profane her nor take her name in vain.

"Father might forgive all else, but this one transgression would never be forgiven. He considers her to be his equal. This is why the earth was patterned after heaven.

"Woman was put on the earth to be man's equal, to stand by his side and to be a helpmate for him. If this were not so, then man wouldn't need the woman to enter the Celestial Kingdom. Man cannot enter the Celestial Kingdom without the woman, nor the woman without the man. Neither is complete without the other."

"I've always felt like that," I said. "I've surely seen a lot of abuse though. Sometimes you'd think men and women were at war with each other."

"Every person will have to answer dearly for his abuses. Father will deal very harshly with them on the day of judgment."

Denial of Entry Another Form of Hell

I looked at the city, shimmering in the celestial light. "I can't bear to be within its sphere of radiance any longer," I said. "I can see where this would really be hell. After seeing this and then knowing I could never enter would be more than I could accept. That would be an eternal hell for me."

We Inherit the Kingdom
For Which We Abide The Laws

"Just remember," said Larry, "we stop ourselves, not God. We've only to live by his laws to inherit his kingdom. Any compromise on our part only brings us partial exaltation. We live only by the laws we're willing to accept."

"If we live a terrestrial law, we will inherit a terrestrial kingdom. If we live a telestial law, we will inherit a telestial kingdom. And if we live by the celestial laws, then we will inherit the celestial kingdom and will stand side by side with Father."

A View of the Landscape

Larry and I rose and began floating gently away. I kept turning to look back at the city as the distance steadily increased. Somehow the radiance didn't seem to diminish, and what I'd just seen remained very vivid in my mind.

"It leaves you with a lasting impression once you've seen it, doesn't it?" asked Larry.

I felt awed, still struggling to find the words which eluded me. I could only nod my head in somber affirmation.

For now, we journeyed in silence as we gently soared above the heavenly landscape below. The beauty of the wooded hills, placid lakes, and gently gurgling streams we crossed filled me with inspirational reverence. Parks, pavilions and stadiums dotted the landscape below.

Other Worlds To See and Explore

"There is so much to see," I remarked to Larry. "It seems like it goes on forever."

"I guess you could say it does," He said. "Besides all that you've seen so far, there are also other worlds to see and explore. There are worlds without number to more than satisfy the most ardent adventurous spirit in each of us."

"I seem to recall seeing some of these worlds before," I said. "It's pretty vague, as though it happened once in a dream."

"Your memory's coming back pretty fast. You'll have no trouble stepping back in again and picking up where you left off," Larry said.

Maybe I wouldn't have any problems, but was I ready for this? I thought. It seemed I'd left too much undone to just pick up where I'd left off.

We began to descend, our speed slowing as a large park appeared.

12

Meeting My Family

Relatives Assembled to Meet Me

"Remember when I told you I had a surprise for you? It's waiting for you there in the park," Larry said, indicating the park ahead.

We settled to a comfortable stop at the entrance. Inside, a large group of people was assembled several hundred yards ahead. They had been talking among themselves in small clusters, but they stopped and turned to face us at our approach, as if they had been expecting us.

"This is your surprise," said Larry, gesturing toward the people. "These are all your relatives. They have all lived on the earth before you. They've all gathered to meet you and to welcome you back."

"So many of them," I said. "I had no idea there were so many of them."

A young woman broke away from the group and started in our direction.

"You'll be in good hands here," said Larry. "I'll call for you later." He waved as he rose and headed away from the park. I watched him disappear and then turned to face the young lady approaching me.

Her long silky robe fluttered gently around her feet as she crossed the grass toward me. She was absolutely beautiful. Her complexion glowed with angelic beauty. Her hair was raven black, which helped to outline her delicate features. Her skin appeared soft and creamy. She was very close to me now. Her robe shimmered with a radiance that dimmed the countenance of the others around her.

Only a Temporary Robe

I felt very conspicuous and uncomfortable as I compared my robe with hers. Mine seemed so drab and gray. I desperately wanted to run and hide so no one could see me. I didn't want to stand next to her and bring more attention to the already garish appearance of my robe.

Words began filling my mind, abating my fears and helping me to reconcile my feelings.

"Don't be concerned with the appearance of your robe. It's only temporary. The visual state of your progression is not to be known at this time. Your permanent robe will be given you later."

My Sister Wendy,
Who Died Before Accountability

I felt better, but I still felt a little awkward as this beautiful woman approached me. She beamed as she spoke my name.

"Larry, Larry! I'm so glad to see you. We've all been waiting for you." She slipped her arms around my neck as she hugged me enthusiastically.

"Don't you know me?" she asked, stepping back so I could see her again. She still held my hands in hers as she leaned back so that I might better view her. Her radiant smile and exuberant personality helped to put me at ease.

"I don't think I do," I stammered.

"It's me, your sister! I'm Wendy! Don't you remember?"

"You're Wendy? But Wendy was just a baby when she died!" I said.

"That's right. I was only three days old when I died. That must be why you don't know me."

We Return to the Spirit World as Adults

"But how is it you're a grown woman?" I asked.

"It was only necessary that I take a body. That's all the time I was given," she explained. "When we die, we return here in our adult form, just like before we were born."

"I'm sorry I acted the way I did when I first saw you," I said.

"What way is that?" she asked, a little puzzled.

"Well, you're just so beautiful," I said, "and your robe is so bright. It's brighter than anyone else's I've seen since I've been here. I just felt so ashamed of mine. I didn't want you to see me dressed like this."

"Don't worry," she said. "It's only temporary."

"That's what I heard when you came over. Why is yours so bright?" I asked.

"We understand they are considering giving you a second chance," she said. "Don't feel bad about your robe. Your permanent one is being kept from you until they make a decision about you."

Robe's Brightness
Reflects One's Level of Glory

She hesitated a moment and then went on. "You see, Father knows the intentions and the purity of our hearts. He has said that all spirits who are born into the world and then die before they reach the age of accountability, that is eight years of age, are without sin. All children who die in this state automatically inherit the Celestial Kingdom.

"Because of my progression, I was only required to take a body. I didn't have to live out a long probationary period on the earth. As far as the countenance of my robe, it reflects the degree of glory I have obtained in the Celestial Kingdom."

Those From Higher Kingdoms
Can Visit Lower Kingdoms

The visions of the Celestial City I saw overwhelmed me as I asked her, "How is it possible you are here with me then? I saw the city from a distance and was told we couldn't go there until we had reached that degree of perfection, and yet you're here?"

She smiled at me understandingly. "If you've not attained Celestial Glory, you can't exist in the Celestial Kingdom nor abide Father's glory unless he has changed you, allowing you to be in his presence without perishing.

"Father will not permit the unworthy to enter the Celestial Kingdom, but those of the higher kingdoms can visit the lower kingdoms. When I knew you were here, I wanted to see you."

Meeting My Family

I looked at the people still waiting. "They're all related to me?" I asked.

"Yes," she said. "We wanted a reunion so we could meet you and let you get to know us. They're all eager to meet you." She slipped her arm in mine as she led me to my waiting relatives.

Intimate Acquaintance Through Embraces

I was embraced fondly by each person I was introduced to as they put their arms around me. With each embrace, an immediate interaction took place between us. A panoramic view would flash through my mind of the experiences each individual had gone through in their lifetime. In this way I came to know each one intimately.

With each person, I found how the family thread tied us together and where on the family tree I was in respect to that person. I wondered how it was that I could be related to so many people.

After I had been introduced, Wendy and I wandered arm-in-arm among the crowd. They had gathered into small groups, talking among themselves. We stopped to swap stories with each group as we encountered them.

"We understand you might get a chance to go back?" I was being asked repeatedly.

"Yes" I said, as I told them of my session with the council and that they were considering my request. "It was wonderful, though," I added, "that they have allowed me enough time to meet with everyone like this before deciding on my request."

Requests to Check Family Lines Back on Earth

The group wanted to know certain things about my family and some of the things that had been happening lately. I answered their questions as best I could.

"If they do let you go back," they concluded, "would you please check on our family history lines?" Some work had been done for them, but there was much more that needed to be done. "We have all worked very hard to complete our genealogical research here. We need to have the rest of the work done on earth before we can progress any further," they said. "If you do go back, could you please remember and check for us? We would forever be indebted to you."

"I'll try," I said. "But I've been told there's a possibility I might not be able to remember anything." I assured them that if I could remember, I would do what I could.

Small groups were now breaking away. Some of them were leaving by themselves, while others were engaged in conversations as they departed.

"You look wistful," said Wendy, still clutching my arm.

"I wonder where they are going?" I said. "You don't know how my heart aches with a desire to follow them and stay here. After everything I've seen, I can't bear the thought of not being able to remember any of it. And you! Meeting you has been one of the greatest thrills I can think of. I'll never be able to think of you as a tiny baby again. In fact, I don't think I'll ever be able to forget you."

Earth Life But a Few Moments to Them

"Thank you," she said. "You're sweet. But if you do go back, just remember that in the twinkling of an eye you'll be back here. Your time there will seem but a few moments to us. It really does pass by quickly."

I wanted to stay so badly, but I had made promises—promises that meant more to me than staying. If I could go back, Georgia and I could be sealed in the temple. Then, when we did cross over again, our progression wouldn't be delayed. Our path to the Celestial Kingdom would be opened for us if we only lived up to the commitments we would be required to make.

Wendy kissed me on the cheek as she hugged me goodbye.

"Larry is here for you," she said as she hugged me one last time and then slipped from my grasp.

As I turned, Larry was just entering the park. I looked back as Wendy waved goodbye.

Larry patiently waited as I struggled to regain control of my emotions. I was deeply touched by the profound effect Wendy had on me as I kept remembering her sweet, tender smile.

13

Peter, James, and John

A Difficult Choice

Well, now what? I sighed.

"Yours is not an easy choice to make," Larry said.

"No, it isn't. It's just . . . it's just . . . ." How could I explain what I was feeling? "It's just that if I were dead, I mean, with no chance of going back, it would be easier. If I could just get control of my feelings and go on from here, it would be so much better

"I know what's facing me back on earth, especially now, after everything you've shown me and after meeting all my relatives and all. It's so hard to go back after seeing and being part of it all. And yet, everything I lived and struggled so hard for is still back there: Georgia, my eternal love; the kids; and all the promises I've made. I have to go back."

I swallowed hard, struggling with my emotions again. Larry moved in closer, trying to console me.

"I understand what you're going through," Larry said. "Like I said, it's not an easy choice."

"Well, now what?" I sighed.

"I've been told to tell you the council is in session and they are requesting your presence. I think they've made a decision."

Remembering the Experiences

My attention was not with Larry, nor on our destination as we left the park. In my mind, I was reliving the experiences again of crossing over and my journey through that "Hell," and of meeting the being of light and seeing the gross earthiness stripped from me. I relived again how I felt when I saw my name being written into the book after I had been directed into the receiving room, and then finding out Larry was to be my guide. I remembered how overjoyed I was to see him. Yes, how truly different he was now than when he was alive.

My throat choked up. I was overwhelmed by my emotions again as I remembered seeing the pure golden light and being told that it was the glory of God. I experienced again the same feelings of love and security that I felt the first time I experienced the pure essence of his love.

I also remembered the look on each council member's face as I implored them, so emphatically, to reconsider and send me back. How badly I had wanted to go back and yet, here I was, torn emotionally over the possibility of returning.

I tried again to visualize the concepts Larry had explained to me when we visited the learning centers. What marvelous opportunities we were afforded to gain knowledge!

I remembered the impact I felt as the genealogical implications had been explained to me, especially now in light of the fact I had just met my relatives.

The view of the heavenly landscape and the other sights I saw as we soared overhead kept flashing through my mind.

I remembered how in awe I had been when I saw the Celestial City, and how I had struggled to sort out feelings I still couldn't comprehend. They were somewhat the same feelings I felt when I first saw Wendy in the park and compared the brilliance of her radiated glory with the brilliance of the Celestial City. It had left me feeling inadequate and inferior, especially when I had learned of her celestial status.

I recalled the reunion in the park and how the lives of each family member, their deeds and misdeeds, were opened up to me. And if that wasn't enough, I remembered finding out also that each individual's garments were a visual indication to everyone of their spiritual progression. It was unsettling to me to think that my own level would be open to such public display.

I still remembered the pleading expression in everyone's eyes as they requested me to please remember them and to check their genealogical research for them. Their insistence, as they instilled in me their desire to have their temple work done for them, left me with a feeling of vague uneasiness. I was troubled by this because it helped to highlight the possibility of my return.

Larry's stopping had brought me back to my present situation. I had been so engrossed in thought I hadn't noticed how we had gotten here.

Meeting the Council at the Stadium

"We're here. The council is waiting for you inside," he said, pointing to the entrance to what looked like a Roman Coliseum or stadium.

Everywhere I looked there were clouds. It seemed the stadium itself was being supported by colossal, cotton-candy-like clouds.

I wished I had paid more attention to how we had gotten here. I looked at Larry with reluctance. I had made my decision though and wasn't going to back out now. Larry said he would wait for me. I hesitantly walked into the stadium.

Ten feet inside, I stopped. The stadium was constructed in two semicircles, with tiered bleachers facing each other and open at either end. The whole stadium appeared to be made of the same crystallized white, marble-like substance as all the other buildings I had seen.

I looked to my left and studied the council members seated there. There were twelve of them. They were talking quietly among themselves in groups of twos and threes.

I looked carefully and studied each group, trying to discern from their faces my possible fate. After studying them thoroughly, I looked to my right at the remaining members. There were twelve men here also. They too were engaged in conversation with each other in groups of twos and threes. Again I could not judge their reaction regarding myself from their faces.

This group of men seated in the bleachers were not the same ones I had met with earlier when I pleaded my cause for wanting to be sent back to the earth.

I realized the council I talked to was simply one of the subordinate groups. They didn't have the authority to grant me my request and send me back.

Different councils were organized for different purposes. There were so many areas of responsibility and interest that responsibility had to be delegated to different councils. Each was under direction and responsibility from a council which had authority over them. I have learned the same organization exists within the church.

Peter, James and John

Straight in front of me was a six-foot-square marble platform about a foot high. Three men were standing on the platform in a close huddle. Two of the men were bent over slightly, facing each other. The third man was between them with his back to me. He was hunched over, with his arms around the shoulders of the other two.

I walked to within ten feet of the platform and stopped. Again, I studied the council members, trying to gain some insight. As if on cue, they all stopped talking at the same moment and turned to face the three men on the platform.

The three straightened up and turned to face me. The man on my left was a slightly built man who was partially bald. His remaining hair was dark. He wore no beard. His robe hung halfway between his knees and ankles and was partially opened down his chest revealing smooth skin without body hair. His arms hung lightly at his side.

The man on my right stood about the same height but was stockier. He sported a full head of black curly hair and a short curly beard. His robe hung halfway between his knees and his ankles and was also partially opened, revealing his hairy chest.

The man in the middle stood a good half a head taller than the other two. He also had a full head of curly black hair and a curly beard, but both were heavily streaked with gray. His robe was the same as the other two, hanging halfway between his knees and his ankles and opened half way down his chest revealing a heavy crop of chest hair. All three were barefoot, as was everyone else I had seen so far.

The one in the middle spoke, telling me they were Peter, James and John. I can only guess that the one speaking was Peter, and that James was the slight-built man. John must have been the stockier of the three. I do not know for sure because they weren't introduced individually. I felt a deep reverent respect in the presence of their authority.

Predictions of Recovery

"We have considered your request," he said. "We feel your family has a greater need of you than we do. But you must be warned what to expect. You will mend and lead a full and useful life, but your healing will not be without problems. You will experience a great deal of pain during your recuperation.

"What you will come to understand is this experience will not make you unique or special. You will still be subject to all the trials and temptations of the flesh. You could easily become discouraged and unless you guard yourself carefully, still be led away down to your own destruction.

"Have you thought over carefully the request you have made, and all its implications?"

I thought for a moment of what he had just told me. "Yes, I have," I stated with conviction.

Request Granted With an Embrace

No other words were said. We only looked at each other for the next few moments. He seemed to glide toward me as I wondered what would happen next. His face was without expression as he stopped by my side and turned as he reached out his right arm, cupping my right shoulder in the palm of his hand. He gazed down intently into my eyes for a moment and then pulled me against him affectionately. Then, as I looked deeply into his eyes, he smiled, flashing a beautiful set of pearly white teeth and his eyes twinkled. I knew my request had been granted.

14

Return to Mortality

My accident happened about 12:30 in the afternoon. After working on me and stabilizing me as best they could, the paramedics escorted me by ambulance to the hospital. Dr. Jay Lynn Smith, who was reported at the time to be the best orthopedic surgeon in the state, was on duty at St. Marks hospital in North Salt Lake when my battered body was brought in.

It was late in the afternoon, about 5:30, when I became aware of my surroundings. My return had been so sudden and swift that I was left with a feeling of confusion and disorientation. I didn't know where I was. I raised my head and looked around. It was as though I was looking through an oval window. In the center of my vision things were clear and easily distinguishable, but they became fuzzy and faded to an undiscernable gray toward the edges.

I was lying on an examination table which was tilted up. I looked down when I heard someone say, "Now Mr. Tooley, this is going to hurt, but it's for your own good." A woman dressed in a nurse's uniform knelt at my feet, preparing to insert a catheter tube into me.

I felt immediate sharp and searing pain as she started pushing the tube in. I screamed out in anguish and I tried to reach out and grab her. The pain was excruciating. I was being restrained, held back. I had been strapped down so as to immobilize me. The straps bit into my shoulders as I tried to lunge out at the nurse. The only thing I could move besides my hands was my head, which I thrashed from side to side. Not only was I struggling against the pain she was inflicting on me but also at the anguish of being strapped down, unable to move or fight back. The struggle exhausted me, and I blacked out for a few moments.

When I came to, the nurse was gone. Dr. Smith was standing outside the examination room talking to Georgia, who kept looking worriedly at me. I laid my head back to rest, and when I looked back to the door I could see my mother and father looking in at me. They were soon replaced by my sisters as they took their turns at the door. It seemed I was babbling incessantly, not saying anything in particular. I looked up again when I heard a noise. The Bishop and his two counselors from the ward we had just moved from were entering the room to administer to me.

I began moaning and groaning loudly, shaking my head from side to side. I didn't want them to touch me because I was in too much pain to have them lay their hands on my head.

As they laid their hands on my head I blacked out. I don't know how long I was out, but when I came to, I was alone again. I tried to move, but found I was still restrained. I heard a noise again and looked up to see Bishop Boyer and his two counselors from our new ward entering the room to again administer to me.

"Oh please don't touch me, it hurts too much," I thought. Moaning and groaning again, I thrashed my head from side to side trying to keep my head from being touched. I was still in too much pain. I only wanted to be left alone.

Emergency Operations

I was in such bad shape when they brought me in that Dr. Smith had Georgia contact my family. He didn't expect me to live for very long. He told her my chances of pulling through were extremely slim. If by some miracle I did pull through, he said I would be an invalid for the rest of my life, confined to a wheelchair.

After the X-rays were developed, Dr. Smith rushed me into surgery. The first thing he did was to open the top of both feet.

Every bone had been fractured or broken. My right foot was so bad that he inserted two eight-inch steel pins under the toes to provide an anchor to attach the bones to.

Dr. Smith then opened my left leg, from a point eight inches below the knee up to the base of the knee, and then around and up the side of my leg to about six inches above the knee.

My bones had been shattered so badly that he used stainless-steel plates to wrap around them, with screws driven into the bones. This would provide strength and allow them to heal properly. My left knee had been crushed like an egg shell. Dr. Smith attempted to reconstruct what he could, but the extensive damage caused my leg to bow more than six inches outward.

Dr. Smith pulled my scalp into place, closing the wound with stitches when he decided no permanent damage had been done to my forehead. The crushing blow, though, had caused my eyes to swell shut. All the apparent damage had been taken care of.

Recovery Begins

Recovery to me seemed like a bad nightmare. Each day was like an eternity as I drifted from restless sleep to fuzzy, drugged reality. I was given substantial doses of morphine to keep the pain under control. The waking hours eventually became more and the sleeping hours less as my strength returned and my need for pain killers eased.

The strength gradually returned to my left hand. It was a herculean effort at first to even move my thumb, but after a lot of effort I got to where I could inch my hand up and down my chest with my thumb. The fingers gradually began moving again, slowly at first, into a weak grasp, and eventually with more flexibility and strength to curl around the fingers of my right hand. In this fashion I could reposition my right hand and arm.

As the muscles in my arm strengthened I was able to begin reaching out for things. After about three weeks I could reach the bar suspended above my head. It was attached by cables through pulleys to slings under each knee. I progressed to where I could only use this as a means to reposition myself slightly.

After almost a month, I finally got strong enough that I could move my right arm with relative ease. This was what the doctor was waiting for. He explained I would have to exercise my knees every day. Whenever I felt strong enough, I was to pull on the bar, bending my knees as far as I could. At this point I thought he was crazy. To move them at all was like hitting a sore thumb with a hammer after it had already been slammed in a car door. But move them I must, he emphasized, or I'd never be able to use them again. Not being able to walk again never occurred to me before. With this in mind I said I would do what I could.

Dr. Smith wasn't satisfied with that. "Five or six times a day or more," he stressed.

I glumly shook my head. As he left, I lay there surveying my legs. The knees were grotesquely swollen and misshapen. I cautiously pulled on the bar, generating very little movement for the pain I felt. Beads of perspiration trickled down my face as I clenched my teeth against the pain each time I reached my limit. Even minor exertion easily drained my energy.

Georgia encouraged me every day to try again each time I wanted to give up. In time it became easier to move my legs, but they always stopped at the same point. Trying to force them farther felt like I was breaking them all over again.

My Impromptu Bugs Bunny Impersonation

The nurses were always cheerful and encouraging. They tried to cheer me up every time they came in to see me. The candy stripers were always puttering around, wanting to know if they could straighten up my bed, fluff up my pillows, or give me a massage. Usually I only wanted to be left alone.

I had been in the hospital about three weeks and was in an unusually sullen mood. Georgia had left to go to the cafeteria for something to eat and to make some phone calls. It was about 10:30 that morning and I was dejectedly watching television when the usual candy striper entered the room with one of her girl friends, another candy striper. After their usual request of wanting to do things for me and me saying no, I relented to their persistent persuasion and let them straighten my bed. I was feeling more despondent than usual as I watched the latest Bugs Bunny cartoon on TV with detachment, wishing they would finish so I could be alone.

Suddenly, both girls stopped and looked at me in amazement. I couldn't understand why they were acting so peculiar. They were courageously trying to stifle their giggles as they put their hands over their mouths in a vain attempt to keep a straight face. They kept snickering as they said "excuse me," and they tried to beat each other out the door. As the door closed, I could hear uncontrolled laughter. I pictured them both rolling on the floor, doubled over in hysterics. The laughter faded as they disappeared down the hall, leaving me more curious then ever.

A few minutes later, Georgia came back into the room. My curious expression prompted her to ask me what was the matter. I told her we had some strange people working at the hospital. I told her what the candy stripers had done and wanted her to find out what was so funny. She was gone for almost a half hour. When she returned she couldn't keep a straight face either.

The nurses had explained to her that very active people, like myself, who had been in accidents or were otherwise immobilized like I was, sometimes "flipped out" momentarily. It's as if the brain temporarily short circuits. That's what I had done. I had unconsciously reacted to the stimulus on the TV. The candy stripers told her that for no explainable reason, I had suddenly sat straight up in bed, bringing both hands up under my chin, chewing like bugs bunny and saying, "Uh—What's up, Doc," and just as quickly, I lay back exactly as I was before.

It did break my glum spell as I tried it to see if I could do it. I still wasn't able to raise my right arm at all by itself, so I wasn't sure I believed her. It still gave me a good laugh when I thought about it.

The Leg Casts Are Removed

The next morning two orderlies came in with a gurney. When I asked them what was going on they told me that I was scheduled for surgery and they were there to get me ready. I was too weak to protest. One of them gave me a pre-op shot. It took effect so quickly I hardly felt a thing as I slipped into unconsciousness.

Sometime later, I became sluggishly aware something was happening. I lifted my head when I felt a strong vibration against my foot. The orderlies were trying to cut the cast off my left foot. One of them had a small power saw he was using to split the cast, and the other looked like he had my foot in a head lock. He was wrestling with the cast, trying to split it open.

I panicked when I saw what they were doing. In my dazed state of mind I thought, My god, what are they doing? Anxiety gripped me as I realized, I'm awake. They're operating on me while I'm awake. I carried that feeling with me all through the operation.

I awoke back in my bed, with Georgia by my side. Groggily I looked down to see what had happened. All of the cast had been removed from my legs and feet. They were being supported now by slings placed six inches apart from my heel to my thighs. Seeing the incisions, which were clearly visible now, was too much for me, and I slipped into unconsciousness again.

It was early the next morning when I awoke, feeling miserable. I would have given anything to be able to sleep on my side again. So far I had been flat on my back, unable to move the whole time.

Georgia never reacted visibly to the sight of my scarred legs, or to the two threaded rods protruding from under the toes of my left foot. Instead, she would always bring me a red rose and smile cheerfully. She tried to distract my attention from my battered limbs by informing me of the latest news from home and what the children were doing. My attention was always brought back to my legs, however, when I tried to exercise them.

Pain in my left leg began within a few days, almost imperceptibly at first, but gradually increasing in intensity with each passing day. My leg was slowly swelling. I watched the incision become taut and then begin to split as the swelling increased. No one seemed to notice. I called the nurses' attention to the clear fluid seeping down my leg from the expanding incision.

At first I could get relief by rubbing my leg, but it wasn't long before even that failed to stop the pain. Georgia couldn't stand to see me in any more pain and went to talk to the head nurse on duty. She convinced her to call the doctor to see what could be done. He had been reluctant to give me anything for the pain because, as he explained to Georgia, he had already given me substantial amounts of morphine and was afraid I would become addicted. He relented this time and prescribed another pain shot.

When the nurse walked into my room with the needle, I asked her what that was for. She told me it was for pain. I told her I didn't need a pain shot. Instead, I wanted her to check my leg to find out why it was hurting all the time. She seemed not to hear me, and she kept insisting on giving me the shot. Finally, my patience exhausted, I told her if she got within arm's length of me with that needle, I would take it away from her and give her the shot. I told her to get out of my room and leave me alone if they weren't going to listen to me. She left in a huff.

I knew something had to be done. I studied the slings under my leg. When I slipped my finger under each one I could feel where the cloth was cutting into my skin, leaving deep creases.

Georgia argued with me when I began undoing each sling, saying she didn't think it was a good idea to take them off. I didn't care by then. I only wanted relief from the pressure and the pain. I told her if they weren't going to do anything, then I would have to do it myself. By then, two cloth slings remained, one under my heel and the other under my knee. The pain hadn't stopped yet. Still, I was determined to get relief. I slid the sling under my heel down to where it barely supported my foot. With no relief yet, I began undoing the last one. As it slipped free, a cool wave of relief swept over me as I lay back in bed. It felt so good because the pain had stopped immediately.

Moments later, when one of the nurses stepped in to see how I was doing, she panicked and began bawling me out when she saw what I had done. I told her I didn't care. If they wouldn't listen to me then I would have to do things myself. She stepped out, summoning help from the other nurses. I explained that the slings had cut my circulation off and that was why my leg had been swelling. They smiled to themselves over my headstrong antics as they repositioned the slings.

"You could have done irreparable damage if your leg had fallen," one nurse scolded with mock anger. I didn't care. The relief was worth it.

By this time I had been moved from my semi-private room into the regular ward on the same floor. My guarded condition had improved. I needed interaction with the other patients.

I had been on the new wing only a short time when a policeman walked by. He looked at me momentarily before stepping away from the door. I was still trying to figure out why a policeman would be in the hospital when he returned and came to my bed. He asked me how I was doing. I told him I was doing O.K.

I was wondering if I had done something wrong when he asked me my name. He could tell by the look on my face I probably was intimidated because of his uniform.

When I told him who I was, he introduced himself and explained his reason for being there. He said he wanted to meet me when I was conscious. He had been one of three policemen who had responded with the paramedics when the call came in concerning my accident. He told me he had never seen anyone fight as hard as I had. It had taken three policemen on one arm and three paramedics on the other just to hold me down when they splinted my legs. He couldn't believe anyone my size who was hurt as badly as I was would have the strength to break the splints the way I did. I apologized for giving them so much trouble. He only smiled. He said he was glad that I fought so hard to live and that I was improving the way I was. We talked a few more minutes before he patted me on the shoulder and left. My memory of the actual accident was gone so I could only wonder at his statement. I didn't know I had that kind of strength either.

The Metal Pins Are Removed

It was almost two months after the accident, on a bright sunny morning when Dr. Smith came in to check on me. "Well, how are you doing today?" he asked with his usual grin. It seemed he always had a smile on his face whenever he talked to the nurses about me before coming in to see me.

"Fine," I said as I watched him check my foot. "How does it look today?"

"It looks pretty good. I think it's time to take the pins out. I'll have one of the nurses give you a shot and then we'll take them out."

"That's O.K. Doc. I don't need a shot." What I didn't want was any more shots. I had an aversion to needles which precluded common sense. I was sure I could do without another one.

He only smiled as he explained, "We can do it without any pain medication if you want. It's up to you, but we'll have to strap you down when I take the pins out."

Now I was worried. "Is it going to hurt that much?" I asked.

"Those pins are about eight inches long. Yeah, I'd say it is going to hurt a little. There's only about an inch sticking out, so there's a lot of pin imbedded in your foot."

I thought about all the pain I had already been through and decided a small prick from a needle was better than any more pain, especially if Dr. Smith thought I needed it. "O.K. Doc. Maybe you're right."

He checked again before leaving. Shortly thereafter the nurse returned with a hypodermic. It seems every time someone comes at you with a needle it always looks like it's a foot long. It really isn't, but it sure seems that way. Just as I thought, when she jabbed the needle in, it burned a lot. I was hoping Dr. Smith was right about needing the shot for the pain.

Soon I was feeling the effects. I felt like I was drunk. I slurred my speech when I tried to talk to the nurse, cracking what I thought were hilarious jokes. She only smiled as she took into account the influence I was under.

Dr. Smith returned with a couple of orderlies. He produced an old-fashioned hand drill which he began chucking up to one of the pins in my foot. I was loud and boisterous as I got after him for giving me another of those infernal shots that I hated so much. It was his fault, I told him, for getting me drunk. I couldn't imagine why everyone was getting so tense as the orderly took hold of my leg when Dr. Smith nodded to him that he was ready. I continued making wisecracks as he began cranking with all of his strength. I didn't feel any pain as he extracted the pin.

Dr. Smith was flushed as perspiration beaded and ran in little rivulets down his face, dripping from his chin. Dropping the pin onto the tray, he chucked the other pin into the drill. This time, he cranked as if his life depended on it. I felt a deep burning pain as the pin began to back out. It felt as if he were pulling every nerve in my body out through my foot. I sobered up completely, not feeling the effects of the shot at all. Grabbing the edge of the bed, a low moan slipped between my clenched teeth. Now I knew why Dr. Smith wanted me to have the pain shot. I couldn't imagine what it would have been like without it.

Everyone relaxed as he dropped the other eight-inch pin onto the tray. Dr. Smith wiped his face with a towel the nurse handed him as he put the pins on the night stand beside my bed. "Here, you can have these as a souvenir." The pain subsided almost as quickly as it began.

"Sorry Doc," I said a little sheepishly. "I didn't mean to say what I did."

"It's O.K.," he said. "You did good." After swabbing antiseptic on the bottom of my foot and taping a bandage on, he left.

Georgia looked at the pins as he left. "My gosh. I had no idea they were that long."

"I didn't either," I remarked, feeling a little sick at the thought.

Hydrotherapy

About two weeks after the pins had been removed from my foot, Dr. Smith felt I was ready for hydrotherapy. He felt I was ready to learn to walk again. A large tank of water to buoy my weight, with handrails to hold on to, would aid in the effort.

Georgia kissed me with encouragement as they wheeled me off to therapy that first morning. I looked skeptical at the tank of water, wondering if this was such a good idea. Then, as the attendant helped me out of the wheelchair and onto the edge of the tank, I decided it wasn't a good idea.

"Take your time," he said. "Just see what you can do. Any time you're ready, let me know and you can get back in the chair."

I eased myself into the water, testing its buoyancy. Even with the water to help, it felt like I was stepping on broken glass.

"That's fine," he said. "If you need me, I'll be in the other room. I have to check on something."

Before he left the room, he pushed the wheelchair about six feet from the tank. He gave me no time to protest as he quickly left the room. The end of the ten-foot tank looked almost a mile away. Reluctantly, painfully, step by step, I worked my way to the end of the tank and rested. My legs felt like rubber and my feet were cramping with the effort. Even with my weight supported by my arms, my legs were starting to burn with pain from the exertion of making them do something they had forgotten how to do. I wanted out, but no attendant was available. I had no choice. The only way out was to walk back the way I came.

Each painful step made my gut wrench. Ages later I eased myself up onto the edge of the tank, holding on for dear life. I felt dizzy and unsteady as I tottered on the edge. I felt that I might pass out at any moment. I had to hold on a little longer. Where was that attendant? I was weak and shaky and sick to my stomach. I waited and waited but no one showed.

Holding onto the edge of the tank for support, I finally lowered myself to the floor. Without the buoyancy of the water to help, the weight on my legs was almost more than I could stand. My feet felt like they were on fire. Searing pain, like red-hot pokers, shot through my legs with each movement.

I carefully eased out until I was at arm's length from the tank, still holding on for support. The wheelchair was still a couple of feet away. If I took a calculated lunge, I figured I could just reach the chair. My legs were shaking badly now and my remaining strength was fading fast. I took a deep breath and pushed hard, reaching out with both hands to grasp the arm rest. I tried to steady myself but my legs collapsed under me as I spun slowly, dropping into the chair exhausted. I didn't have enough strength left to straighten myself up.

The attendant, unknown to me, had been in the other room watching me through a two-way mirror. As I dropped into the chair he came rushing in.

"You're all done, I see," he said, half-smiling to himself. "Are you ready to go back to bed?"

I weakly nodded my head as he repositioned me in the wheelchair, covering me up with a warm blanket. The trip up from hydrotherapy to my bed took forever. I kept wondering to myself if we would make it before I passed out from exhaustion and fell out of the chair.

I looked at the bed with gratitude as we arrived. "I'm afraid you're going to have to help me," I said weakly. "I don't have enough strength left even to get out of the chair."

"No problem," he said, carefully lifting me onto the bed. After changing me into a dry, warm hospital gown, he pulled the covers up under my chin and I slipped into a deep sleep. Twelve hours later I awoke for breakfast, feeling somewhat better.

Georgia's Account

Time never seems to move as slowly as when you're in a desperate situation, waiting for something to happen. In my case, the hours waiting for Larry to come out of the operating room dragged on into eternity. The hands of the clock had to be frozen in perpetual slow motion. Each revolution of the second hand took an hour. The well of my tears must have run dry, or so I thought. I desperately wanted to hear that he was going to be all right.

I felt my world would come crashing down around my shoulders if I were left alone. How was I ever going to raise our children by myself? For that matter, how was I going to raise them if he survived? If he lived through this, would he ever be normal again? All I could see was a lifetime with Larry relegated to a wheelchair.

"Please God," I prayed. "Let him pull through this. I need him so much. Even if he is crippled for the rest of his life, at least I'll be able to be with him. I'll do anything you want if I can only have him back."

I don't know how many times I said that prayer or different variations of it. My mind was like a cracked record that kept repeating the same thing over and over again. The knot in my stomach grew tighter each time I assessed the situation.

A wave of relief flooded over me when Dr. Smith stepped into the waiting room. My heart lumped in my throat, jack-hammering against my temples as he walked over to me. His face was emotionless, like a slab of granite, when he sat down next to me.

I couldn't wait for him to speak as I blurted out, "How is he? Is he going to be all right?"

Dr. Smith took my hands in his, in his cool professional manner, his eyes red with fatigue because of the strain he had been under. "We're not out of the woods yet. We still have some serious problems to deal with. If by a miracle he does pull through, he'll be paralyzed for life."

Tears filled my eyes again. I was in a daze as he continued.

"He hit his head pretty hard when he fell. Usually a blow that hard will cause a concussion. If he had hit the back of his head that hard it probably would have affected his motor sensory skills. I won't know the extent of the damage for a few days. He's had compound fractures of both legs. I've braced the bones in his legs with steel because of how badly they were damaged.

"There's been severe damage to both knees. His left knee was so bad it's probably irreparable. The important thing is to keep them mobile. We're rigging trapeze supports above his bed to suspend his legs and also to keep his knees movable. We've put on partial casts for now. If we cast them completely they'll permanently heal in one position. He won't have any movement out of them at all.

"He's fractured or broken every bone in both feet. I've implanted pins into his left foot as an anchor to tie the bones to. It'll be several weeks before we can start him on any kind of therapy.

"I'm putting him in a semi-private room for now. I want to keep all visitations to a minimum. I wouldn't expect much of a reaction out of him. We're keeping him heavily sedated. He'll probably only come around for short periods for a while."

All I could think of was that he was going to live. I listened to the rest of what he said in a daze. I couldn't fight the tears back as he told me how badly he was hurt. He said we could go in to see him but not to make it very long. Larry had to be maintained in a very guarded condition and would have to be watched closely for the next few days.

I was completely drained from emotional fatigue as I held his hand in mine, looking into a face I didn't recognize. Good grief, how could he ever survive, I thought. He looked like he had been hit with a semi-truck. Dr. Smith told me it would probably be hours before he came out from under the anesthesia. It was late and I needed to get home to the children. I kissed Larry goodbye, telling him I loved him and that everything was going to be all right.

It was dark when we all stepped outside into the parking lot. "Keep us informed how he's doing," they said as everyone left.

I don't remember the drive from the hospital to Midvale ever being as long as it was that night. I knew I would have to get used to it because I would be doing it a lot in the months ahead.

My friend, Mary Ann, had done a marvelous job with the children. I wanted to go to bed and sleep for a thousand years but it would be impossible. Even now the twins were crying for attention, wanting to be fed.

My days and nights became a nightmare, one I wished I could wake up from but couldn't. Every night I somehow managed a couple of hours of sleep but nothing more. The children demanded attention, which was a full-time job in itself.

Watching Larry each day struggling to come to grips with the accident was heart-breaking. When he began to be able to communicate with me he talked a lot, not always coherently, but always excitedly. He kept saying things I didn't understand, talking about things he had seen while out of his body, most of which didn't make any sense to me because he wouldn't maintain much continuity. I wondered if he was delirious, considering what he had been through. He kept telling me I was the reason he had come back and that he had seen Larry. He was jumping from one thought to another, making it difficult to understand or even follow what he was saying. At times he would fall asleep in the middle of a sentence, often times picking up where he left off when he woke up. It wasn't long before his rambling stopped.

Somehow, I managed to act as if everything was all right. Larry had enough to worry about without knowing how everything was really going. I couldn't tell him that the older kids couldn't understand why he wasn't coming home anymore. Their insecurity kept them always hanging onto me whenever I was home.

Although he was only six years old, Nathan picked up the slack again, trying to be the man of the house. He had always been protective of me when I was married before. He had been forced to accept responsibility far in advance of his age. Now, with Larry gone, he was having to accept even greater responsibility again.

Three-year-old Lori could only react to something she couldn't understand. I couldn't explain to her about the accident. Her insecurities were only added to by Larry's absence. She had been deprived of her biological father, and now she was being deprived again.

Darren was reacting to the situation around him by always crying. No, screaming was more like it. Julie always followed suit. She must have been thinking if Darren was crying it was for a reason so she would cry also.

They couldn't understand why I would leave early in the morning, sometimes not returning until late at night. I was becoming more and more exhausted with each passing day but for Larry's sake, I had to be there.

After the doctor started Larry on exercise, I would cringe each time he would try to force his knees to move. His knees were so badly swollen I couldn't see how he was able to move them at all. He never said anything, but I could see despair in his eyes as he wiped away the tears as he struggled to make his limbs move.

At first he could only use his left arm to pull with; his right arm refused to respond. Then later, he would lift his right arm with his left so he could pull with both hands. I could tell it wasn't easy. He wanted to give up, but I wouldn't let him. Somehow he had to be all right.

Larry would only listen to reason just so long before he took it upon himself to do something, if he thought no one was responding to his problems.

After they removed all the casts, they put his legs into slings to support them. He kept saying his left leg hurt. I watched as he rubbed it for hours, trying to get the pain to stop. Nothing seemed to work. The nurses didn't seem to think anything was wrong. His leg was swelling so badly I thought it would split wide open. Instead of going down, it kept getting bigger every day.

When he couldn't get anyone to listen to him he began trying to adjust the slings himself. "The circulation is cut off," he kept telling me. I asked the nurse if they could give him something for the pain. "Not without the doctor's orders," was all they could tell me. I finally insisted if they didn't do something, I would. The head nurse finally called the doctor. She put me on the phone at his request. "Georgia, we can't give him any more pain killers. He's had so much now I'm afraid we're going to have an addict on our hands." I told him how much pain he was in and insisted he do something. He finally told the nurse to give Larry a shot.

When we went back into the room and Larry found she had a shot for him, he became angry. "I wouldn't need a shot if you'd only listen to me," he told her. She seemed beyond reason as she insisted on giving him the shot. I only wanted to see him out of the pain. If that's what it took, then that's what it took. Larry finally threatened her if she didn't leave him alone.

She had become angry. I had hounded her to do something and now that she was, Larry was throwing her out of the room. She took her anger out on us after that by enforcing the visitation rules and limiting the number of visitors in the room at any one time.

After the nurse left, Larry began undoing the supports. I begged him not to, for fear something would happen, but he said he didn't care and took them off anyway. He only had one support left under the edge of his heel when he finished but it finally did some good. The pain quit and the swelling started going down.

I was feeling more haggard with each passing day but I refused to stay home. Somehow I managed to drag myself to the hospital every day. It was especially bad at night when I would leave and go home. It was always after dark when I would walk across the parking lot to my car.

One day the nurses told me to be careful leaving at night. One of the nurses had been attacked and raped the night before in the parking lot. That was all I needed, one more thing to have to worry about.

One night, after leaving the hospital, I found I had a flat tire. I was so sure that it was a setup that I drove the car anyway. My sister lived in the Avenues, not far from the hospital. I drove all the way there on that flat tire and spent the night at her place. I got it fixed the next morning. After that I tried to leave while it was still light outside.

When Dr. Smith told me he was going to remove the pins from Larry's foot, I couldn't stand to be in the room. I couldn't imagine having pins like that sticking out of his foot anyway, let alone seeing them removed.

Larry was funny after they gave him a shot for the pain. It must have been very strong, because he began acting like he was drunk or something. If he could have stood on his feet I don't think he could have walked a straight line.

I waited in the hall until they were finished before I went in to see Larry. He wasn't acting like he was drunk anymore. I couldn't believe how long the pins were when Larry showed them to me. "Didn't it hurt when they took them out?" I asked.

"Oh, a little," was all he would say.

I began running a fever shortly after that. Everyone advised me to stay home and take it easy, but I felt I was still needed at the hospital every day. The hectic pace was catching up to me. Then, one morning I couldn't get out of bed. My temperature had risen to 104 degrees. I was in a state of total physical exhaustion.

I can remember my parents wanting to call an ambulance but I wouldn't let them. I begged them to let me stay home. If I could only rest a couple of days I knew I would be all right. My mother agreed only if she could stay with me and take care of the children. If anything changed though, she said they were taking me to the hospital immediately. I was glad for the help, but I knew I had to hurry and get better so I could go back to the hospital. "Please don't say anything to Larry," I begged.

Larry's Account

About a week after I started hydrotherapy, Georgia didn't show up at her usual time. I was relieved to be left alone for a couple of days. It was nice that she could see me all the time, but it was very tiring. I felt as though I needed to be awake all the time, if for nothing else but just to talk to her. I had no way of knowing that she had collapsed from sheer exhaustion because of the demands on her time from the kids and me. She had gone weeks without sleep, and now she was paying the price. This time when she came to see me she didn't stay as long, saying she had to get back to the kids.

Whenever meals would be delivered I would generally pick at my food. Nothing tasted any good. This was not like me. After this length of time, it occurred to me that I should be eating more than just a couple of bites of food. I was skin and bones, as my weight had shrunk to 146 pounds. I was getting worried about my weight loss.

One day, when Dr. Smith was making his daily rounds, he stopped to see me. He was marking my progress on my chart when they brought my medication. By then I had figured out that something had to be affecting my appetite. I asked him if something in one of the pills they were giving me was the reason I wasn't eating. He stopped writing and looked at the pills the nurse had given me.

"If you're smart enough to figure that out, it's time to take you off of them," he said, writing the information on my chart.

"How am I going to get better if I don't start eating and gain some weight back?" I commented, feeling more than a little irritated. Dr. Smith only smiled as he walked out of the room.

Released from the Hospital

About the middle of November, Dr. Smith felt a trial weekend at home was in order. He felt it was necessary to prepare the family and myself for my return home. Not only was I a physical wreck, but my nerves were shattered also.

As the weekend arrived, I was bundled into the car and strapped in with the seat belt for the trip home. Georgia must have thought I had gone crazy. Practically every car I saw would just about make me go to pieces because I was so afraid one of them might hit us. I couldn't stand the thought of any more pain.

I carried that same thought with me as we pulled into the driveway. Georgia had to make sure the kids stayed at least three feet away from me as I worked my way into the house. The hospital had given me a walker to use, which I brought with me. I couldn't walk without it, even though I used it more for a shield so I could keep the world at arm's length. I loved the kids, but I would go to pieces if I thought one of them might bump my legs. I was very relieved when I was returned to the safety and the sanctuary of the hospital bed and the staff.

It was just before Christmas when Dr. Smith released me from the hospital. Weekly checkups were all that was required now.

Georgia's Account

How many times I cried myself to sleep, I'll never know. I lost count somewhere along the way. I used to dream Larry and I were walking hand-in-hand in the park, the way it used to be before the accident. Now that he was released from the hospital, I prayed and dreamed for the day when we could just walk through the malls again.

Maybe I was being selfish, always wanting something just beyond my grasp. Larry was doing reasonably well considering we had earlier faced the prospects of his never being able to walk again.

I mentioned to Larry, on several occasions, my desire to be able to walk with him again, just like old times. Maybe it was because of this desire that Larry wanted to go to the mall with me right after he was released. I asked him if it would be too much for his legs, but he insisted on going anyway, saying he would stop if it became to much for him.

The Christmas decorations and the lights helped to brighten the holiday spirit as we entered Fashion Place Mall. I guess we hadn't realized how crowded it would be just before Christmas. Larry depended heavily on his walker as we slowly worked our way through the crowd. I was worried, watching him trying to navigate through so many people as they crowded shoulder to shoulder, sometimes bumping into his walker.

We had only managed to make it a fourth of the way through when Larry eased himself into the first seat available. He looked fearfully at the never-ending stream of people. It was the same way he looked when I brought him home in November when he was so afraid one of the kids would bump his legs. I could tell it was too much for him. He quickly agreed when I told him we were going home. I really questioned his ability to be able to make it back to the car. I could tell the pain was becoming unbearable the way he gritted his teeth, trying to hold back the tears. Every bench offered an excuse to give his legs a rest as I watched him rub them, trying to ease the pain.

He slumped into the seat, exhausted, as I held the car door open for him. It was foolish for us to attempt to go out so soon after coming home, but his determination to walk was undeniable.

As he slipped into bed after we came home, I realized one of my prayers had been answered. I thanked God that night as I lay there watching Larry sleep. But I knew it was going to be a long time before things would ever get back to being normal.

15

My Pre-Mortal Parting from Georgia

It was the next month, in late January, 1973, when I received my first flashback. It was one of those cold, blustery winter days that makes it feel good to huddle around a warm fire. Almost immediately after the accident I had talked to Georgia about some of the things I had seen, but as the days swiftly passed the memories were fading.

I felt unusually tired and wanted to go to bed early. I had just relaxed, laying back onto my pillow and getting comfortable. Georgia was in the bathroom preparing for bed. I was in that state of total relaxation, midway between sleep and being awake.

Recollection of a Pre-mortal Meeting With Georgia

Suddenly, before my eyes, in all its vivid details, I saw the last meeting I had with Georgia, just before I was born. I saw myself at the point in time when I had just been informed that my time to be born on the earth had arrived. I recalled that there was much to do and so many preparations to make, yet there was so little time to do it. I could feel the impatience growing in me. I knew what I had to do first. I thought of Georgia, my beloved. I wanted to share my excitement and good news with her.

Thought-guide Travel Through the Universe

My desire intensified as I formed an image in my mind of where she was. I began moving with increasing speed. It seemed only moments before the lights around me winked out as I broke the light barrier. Here and there, a speck of light blinked on, then off as a star sped by. What a wonderful power we possessed to move through the universe. Time and space were no barriers. We had only to think of where we wanted to go and we would be there. Thought was faster than light.

Suddenly, light flooded the universe again as my speed dropped. Ahead lay my destination as a speck before me grew in size. This speck quickly became a world as my speed continued to slow.

A Beautiful Meadow

I glided to a gentle stop under a large tree. A beautiful, rolling meadow of velvety green grass stretched out before me. Wild flowers of all descriptions and colors grew in splendid profusion. Large, stately trees offered shadowed light beneath their boughs. The air was pure and vibrant. Rolling, sloping hills rose gently in the distance away from me.

Hundreds of Children Playing

Tiny children, numbering in the hundreds, were gleefully running about. I watched a small group playing tag. Others were running hand in hand, giggling and laughing as they went.

I could see Georgia holding hands with fifteen or twenty children as they danced in a circle, playing something like ring-around-the-rosy. I was content to stand and watch, feasting on her beauty. It seemed I had never seen her more beautiful or alive than at that moment.

Pre-mortal Georgia Described

She was so elegant and graceful, she looked like a victorian goddess. Her long hair hung in ringlets over her left shoulder. Her long, white dress hung gracefully from her right shoulder, leaving her left shoulder bare as the dress draped across her left breast. She was barefoot, as were all the children. Her long eyelashes couldn't conceal her beautiful deep green eyes. She radiated with a glow of internal beauty.

She beamed as she sensed my presence and turned to see me standing under the tree. She excused herself from the children and came to me, taking my hands in hers.

"We need to be alone. Come with me to our special place. I have something important to tell you," I said.

Travel to Our Special Garden Place

We took one last look at the children. Turning, we formed the image of our garden home in our minds. I held her hand tightly as we sped off, quickly exceeding the speed of light. The lights of the stars winked on and off as we sped through space. Just as quickly, our speed slowed, dropping us back into sub-light speeds.

A speck before us grew, quickly forming into a world as our speed continued to slow. We gently came to a stop in a beautiful glen by a stream. Rolling hills ran in every direction. A soft, velvety green, mossy path followed the edge of the stream.

The stream trickled by, making small ripples as Georgia and I walked hand-in-hand down the path. Golden rainbows in the mist above danced from water droplet to water droplet around us. Peace and tranquility wafted through the still air.

"It's so beautiful," she said. "I wish we could spend eternity here. I really love it. It's no wonder I don't ever want to leave it."

"This will always be our garden, our special place," I said. "This was created for no one else but us."

A large flat rock flanked the stream ahead. It angled, slopping into the stream.

"Let's stop there," I said, gesturing toward the rock.

Georgia seated herself, wrapping her arms around her knees, leaning forward. As I knelt in the grass beside her, I could feel my emotions rising inside me. I faltered, searching for the words, trying to gauge the depth of her reaction by her expressions.

Information Given About Their Earthly Births

"I've . . . I've been informed it's my time," I said quietly.

The light flickered in her eyes and they became misty.

"How wonderful!" she said. "It's been so long. I can't believe it's finally going to happen. How soon will you be leaving?" she asked.

"Very soon. They said the time was almost at hand," I replied.

She looked away, trying to hide her feelings. "Have they said anything about me?" she asked.

I could feel her apprehension as I reached out, turning her face to me.

"Yes," I said. "It will be very soon afterwards. In earth terms, probably just a couple of years. Geographically we'll be close, but it will probably be years before we find each other."

"Won't there be problems?" she asked, her eyes pleading. "I'm so afraid we'll never be together again. I just don't think I could accept that."

Arrangements Made to Meet on Earth

I tried to reassure her. "Yes, I'm sure there will be problems. That's why I've made arrangements for things here."

"In our altered consciousness, we could forget completely about each other. Why, we'll probably wind up married to someone else and then we'll never find each other. We'll never be together again," she said, her eyes growing dark.

"That's why I've made special arrangements here, before we go over. When the time is right, we'll be drawn together," I said.

"What good will that do?" she asked. "We still won't know each other."

I took her hands in mine. Our eyes met as I said, "I'll know you. I need only to look into your eyes and I'll know who you are. I could never forget your eyes." I paused, then stated with conviction, "I'm sure things will probably happen once we're on the earth. That's why I've taken precautions here. I will find you, and when I do, I know I'll be hard pressed to convince you to marry me. I know it will take awhile, but I will convince you. When I do, we'll be married.

A Promise of Temple Marriage

"I'll make this promise to you now," I said. "After we're married and we complete all the necessary preparations, I'll take you through the temple and make you my queen. We'll be sealed together for time and all eternity."

The mist in her eyes spilled over, wetting my cheek as I held her close. The only sound that came to our ears was the trickling of the stream. I lifted her to her feet as we linked arms, her head resting softly on my shoulder as we strolled arm-in-arm though our personal Garden of Eden.

Magnificent trees shrouded the distant, misty hills. Delicate, floating water lilies bobbed gently in the water. Beautiful flowers grew in stately splendor, filling the air with their fragrance. We etched every detail indelibly in our minds. It would be a long time, we knew, before we would return.

Back to the Present: The Recollection Shared

When Georgia came out of the bathroom, she was alarmed by the expression on my face as she rushed to my side.

"What's the matter?" she asked with alarm.

She listened as I recounted the details of the experience that had just unfolded before my eyes. She listened, enthralled, as I described in intimate detail the way she had appeared to me—a victorian goddess of pure celestial beauty, encircled by ethereal glory—as we said our last farewell.

How different it was to see her in this new light, for me to know where my feelings came from and to be able to make the tie-in.

16

Eternal Goals Completed

Ordination and Blessings

I dogged Bishop Boyer relentlessly after that experience. Now it was more important than ever that the final preparations be made for us to go through the temple.

The final requirements were met as he conferred the proper priesthood authority on me, which opened the way for us to enter the temple to exchange eternal vows.

Still, another matter of importance needed to be taken care of first. Julie and Darren needed to be blessed. Nathan and Lori were also lacking in this department.

Arrangements were completed, and on the first Sunday in February, 1973, those blessings and ordinances were performed in Sacrament Meeting. After the normal church business had been taken care of, the time was turned over to me.

I proudly rose, first taking Darren in my arms and walking, unaided, down the aisle to the front of the chapel. I had been doing a lot of walking up to now and my legs had been getting stronger. I had finally gotten to where I could navigate without the walker for short distances. Even though my damaged left knee bowed out, making walking difficult, I was determined to complete my labor of love. But every step put extra strain on the outside of my left knee, causing me pain.

The bishopric and all other requested members gathered around, each helping to support Darren as we formed a circle of power and authority. A hush fell on the congregation as I bestowed a blessing on him worthy of his heavenly heritage.

Patiently, in silence, everyone waited as I made my way down the aisle to give Darren to Georgia and take Julie in my arms. The stand at the front of the chapel looked like it was a block away as I started down the aisle again. Even though it was becoming increasingly more painful with each step, I wouldn't think of stopping. Again, we stood encircled as a blessing was imparted with the power and authority of the priesthood.

I gently laid Julie in Georgia's arms as all eyes rested on me. Reaching out for Lori, she proudly took my hand as we made our way down the aisle. It was more difficult this time and I had to walk a little slower, but this was our moment. Every step was aided by the silent support of the members. Lori sat quietly as we crowded around to lay our hands on her head and give her a special blessing. Afterwards she sweetly led me back down the aisle, for now it was Nathan's turn.

He eagerly joined me as I struggled down the aisle for the last time. Fatigue was clearly showing on me, but nothing on earth was going to prevent me from completing my task of love. But I had no idea it was going to be so hard to walk up and down the aisle so many times.

Nathan reverently bowed his head as the combined powers of the priesthood bestowed their authoritative blessing upon him. Elation crowded out the pain as I struggled, this time with great difficulty, back down the aisle. I don't think I could have made it one more time. We took our seats as a proud family.

Everyone exchanged handshakes of congratulations after the meeting. But I was not through yet. I couldn't rest until I had gotten Bishop Boyer to complete the arrangements for Georgia and me to go through the temple.

An Operation to Repair my Shoulder

Shortly after this, Dr. Smith made arrangements for me to be fitted with a long leg brace. This would give the needed support to my left leg. Until now, as I walked, my weight rested on the outside of my left knee, which was causing me increasing distress. This brace helped matters immensely, but it caused me to walk stiff-legged because it would lock into place whenever I stood up.

Dr. Smith also had been concerned that I hadn't gotten the full use in my right arm back yet. He wanted to go back in for exploratory surgery to see if anything was wrong. The prospect of going back into the hospital wasn't appealing, but the idea of not gaining full movement in my arm again didn't appeal to me either.

By now the new St. Marks hospital had been completed on Thirty-ninth South and Fifth East in Salt Lake City. The old hospital out near the northern Salt Lake City boundary had been closed down. Even though the facility was newer, it still didn't make me feel any better lying in bed waiting to go into surgery. Georgia kept reassuring me it was for the best, trying to make me feel better.

I was admitted into surgery the next morning. It seemed only a short time before I began coming out from under the anesthesia. As usual, Georgia was there holding my hand when I came to. I couldn't feel any pain this time. I was wondering if he had done anything until I noticed an elastic sleeve over my arm with a sling around my neck. Then I noticed the bandages over my shoulder.

It would take time, I knew, before I could use my arm again. For the moment, I only wanted to get out of the hospital. Several hours later Dr. Smith came into the room to inform us what he had found. Too much time had passed since the accident before anything had been done. Torn ligaments and muscles hadn't shown up on any X-rays. Everyone had just thought that I had pulled the muscles in my arms when I had been wrenched loose from the beams, and that they would naturally get better on their own. He found this was not the case as he tried to stretch the ligaments back into place and reattach them. Torn muscles had been repaired as best he could in the operation.

After landing feet first and then collapsing onto my knees, I had pitched forward onto my right shoulder before hitting my forehead. He had to cut out part of the rotator cuff that had been damaged. When my arm had been pulled out of the socket, the muscles in my chest, neck, and back had all been torn loose.

He stated that he didn't think I would ever regain full use of my arm again. Exercise might help to strengthen it, though. I was released from the hospital several days later to finish recuperating at home.

We Become an Eternal Family

It was shortly after this that Georgia and I received final approval to go through the temple. Bishop Boyer smiled as he handed us our temple recommends. It was with deep gratitude that we accepted them. We eagerly set the date. What a wonderful feeling we shared, knowing that we were about to accomplish our eternal goal: to be married and sealed as husband and wife for all eternity.

On May 14, 1973, we gathered outside the Salt Lake Temple. We made last-minute checks and adjustments, trying to quiet the worst case of butterflies in recorded history. Temple recommends ready? Kids ready? Were we ready? We looked at each other and sighed. Yes, we were ready.

Proudly, we handed our temple recommends to the attendant who was expecting us. We were ushered in and directed to an office for final instructions. The children were attended to until the proper moment came in the ceremony.

From that moment on I was not to see Georgia or be with her until the completion of our personal endowments and our entry into the celestial room of the temple. We quietly basked in the reverence of this historic building, feeling the heavenly peace it afforded as it represented to us a heaven on earth.

We were ushered into a sealing room as the presiding authority took charge. Georgia and I faced each other from opposite sides of the room as the aspects of our temple marriage were explained. Eternal principles were revealed eloquently, and the officiator elaborated on the heavenly side of the promises we were making and the covenants we were participating in.

Now, Georgia and I rose, crossing to the altar in front of us. As we were directed, we kneeled, joining hands over the altar. The marriage ceremony began.

Here again, I was holding hands as before with my eternal love and companion. I repeated the words as I looked deeply into those same beautiful, emerald-green eyes that had held me spellbound since the beginning of time.

As our celestial marriage ceremony was completed I kissed her. Tears flowed freely as our emotions overflowed.

Now came the second part as the children, dressed in white, were brought in and presented to us. Kneeling again across the altar, we were sealed, in the eyes of God and the angels, for all time and for all eternity, as husband and wife, parents and children—an eternal family unit, partaking together of glorious promises and blessings in the celestial order of things.

17

Torn Between Heaven and Earth

An Operation to Straighten My Leg

Several months after Georgia and I had gone through the temple, Dr. Smith asked us to come to his office for a conference. After checking everything out he said he had a solution to suggest concerning my bent leg. I might not have to wear a brace anymore.

He said he had been studying all the X-rays and he thought that by going back in and removing the steel he could take a wedge out of the bone. This, in effect, would bring my leg straight, allowing my weight to be supported straight down on the knee instead of my leg having to bear all my weight on the outside as it was doing now. The steel, of course, would have to be put back around the bones for support.

I was apprehensive at the prospect of going back into the hospital one more time. He understood how I was feeling and he explained that the choice was up to me. If I kept things the way they were, my knee would eventually wear out and I would have to have it replaced with an artificial one. If I went ahead with the operation and I was careful, I would probably get by for years, probably for the rest of my life without too much difficulty.

It was depressing to think about going back into the hospital one more time, even with the prospect of being able to walk normally again. I gave it a lot of thought and earnest prayer before Georgia and I decided the best course of action would be to go ahead with the operation.

The arrangements were made, and I checked into the hospital. I spent several hours staring at my legs, and I remembered when I had taken such things for granted. The many months since the accident seemed like a lifetime. Even though it had been extremely painful, I had come to accept my deformity. As I lay in bed, it took little effort to think back over the previous months of surgery and the pain and anguish I had endured to get to where I was. Now I was faced with several more months of therapy.

After the operation it was strange to look at my legs and see them straight again. The stigma that I had been afflicted with had been removed successfully. Walking wasn't easy at first, but it was easier by far than when I was first learning to walk after the accident.

To fulfill workmen's compensation requirements, Dr. Smith evaluated me, determining that I was sixty-two-and-a-half percent disabled for life. From all outward appearances I'm normal, although I have struggled through the years to find ways of doing things that everyone else takes for granted.

How My Near-death Experience Has Influenced My Life

Many years have passed since I first had my near-death experience. I have relived one or more aspects of that experience almost every single day of my life since then.

I find I live in two different worlds. The first is my life here in mortality where I get up every morning, go about my normal routine, go to my job every day and pursue my temporal interests.

The other is the spirit world where every day I make comparisons between this mortal life and the glorious things I observed beyond the veil. I cannot deny what I saw and experienced. To do so would be to deny my knowledge of the existence of God, or even to deny my own existence.

One of the greatest driving forces since my experience I've had to live with is a sense of urgency, of not having enough time to complete things. I've felt that I could be taken away at any moment and it is extremely important not to leave any task undone.

It's been difficult living with my experience, not only from my point of view, but also from my family's perspective. I've read in books and newspaper accounts that between 80 and 85 percent of the people who have had near-death experiences have divorced or separated from their spouses. I can understand why. Some people can't relate to their spouse's experiences. They feel that his or her near-death experience violates pre-conceived ideas they have about death and heaven.

While generally positive, a near-death experience typically "leaves people with an intense longing to return" to that other world. When I would talk to Georgia about what I had seen and experienced, it was with such an intensity, and longing for the tranquility and freedom I felt there that it disturbed her. From the very first days after the accident, Georgia has been aware of the things I saw and heard. She even heard my incoherent ramblings about the experience before I had recovered enough to be clear and lucid about them. But they worried her. It finally came out one day that she was afraid that I might commit suicide in order to leave and go back.

It utterly surprised me that she would have this fear. To me it was a beautiful experience and something to share. It gave answers to many of the questions we have about death and what lies beyond, and also what happened before we were born. We may be homesick for our other life, but not so much that we would rush our own death. All who have had a near-death experience and who have been sent back to earth know that we're sent back to fulfill a very real and specific purpose in this life.

While there is a longing to die on some people's part who have had near-death experiences, most feel very strongly against suicide and know that it is forbidden. We are not afraid of death, and we know first-hand what a beautiful experience life beyond the veil really is.

Most of us will relate that there is no pain associated with death. What little pain is felt before dying, by some, is quickly forgotten and crowded out by the overwhelming joy and peace they experience.

Those who have experienced near-death episodes try to recapture many of the sensual aspects of the experience. Some go to paint stores and pan through hundreds of paint chips, looking for the dazzling array of colors they saw. Some try amusement park rides to experience a similar sense of movement. There are those who have musical abilities who have been able to recreate the music they heard while in the other world.

Senses such as hearing, touch and sight seem to be enhanced. Some people report an "unusual magnetic activity around them." They can no longer wear digital watches. Others, because of this magnetic activity, have found that they have unusual healing powers that defy medical science.

For some, things like cars, homes, travel and achievement now seem mundane and foolish. For most of us, the experience is played over and over in our minds "like a never-ending loop." Some have found it difficult to cope with the normal routines of mortal life.

I have had the joy and sense of accomplishment of being able to overcome most of my infirmities associated with my accident. It has taken years, in some instances, and in others I've had to immediately come to grips with some of my worst fears and phobias.

Because of the understanding of my wife and her strong moral fiber, I have been able to watch my children grow and mature into healthy adults. We have instilled in them the attitude that the word "can't" doesn't exist. They can accomplish anything they have a desire to do.

Life is full of challenges. Some challenges are met with failure, others with success. Failing at something is not necessarily wrong. In failing they have learned they either failed because they hadn't tried hard enough or else weren't prepared enough to succeed. Regardless, all experiences have been educational and have taught them patience and prepared them for adult life.

I have been able to see in them the spiritual side of their nature. Because I have been allowed to remember my pre-mortal life to some degree I have been able to see them grow into a mirror image of their spiritual personalities. I can appreciate to some degree their struggles and aspirations. This is not to say that I have always been as patient as I should have been with them, but Georgia has been the moderator in the family. She has always tempered the differences between us and has been able to bond us into a cohesive family unit.

Under her direction and guidance, our children now lead successful lives and have learned the value of a good education. As I watch them now, I can see that they have the same desires for their children as I have for them.

18

Other Glimpses Beyond the Veil

O ne very important, and quite typical, aspect of having participated in a near-death experience is that I find the veil between life and death to be much thinner for me now. I have sometimes been allowed to see individuals who have left mortality and observe their actions for brief intervals. Let me relate several such experiences.

Mother-in-law
Seen Attending Her Own Funeral

The years have taken their toll in respect to our loved ones. I have struggled with my emotions as I attended the funeral of Georgia's mother, June Newbold. She died on February 4, 1980, and was buried in Valley View Memorial Cemetery in West Valley City, Utah.

When the family gathered at the viewing to participate in the family prayer, I could see her spirit standing beside the one giving the prayer. Apparently no one else was able to see her there except for me. She was beautiful. I also had a glimpse of her several hours before the funeral and could see her getting her hair done, and I observed how beautifully she was dressed.

She was at peace with herself. How I envied her. Seeing her brought back my own memories more vividly than ever.

She Kissed Each Family Member Goodbye

After the family prayer, we all filed into the chapel for the rest of the services. The family was seated on the first row with the casket resting in front of us. The speakers stood at the podium giving their eulogies, which gave me a few moments to close my eyes. She was still there, only now she was moving from person to person. When she came to each family member she stopped, bent forward, and kissed each one on the forehead. It was her way of saying goodbye to the family.

She Prompted Words at the Dedication of the Grave

Later, at the grave site, as the grave was being dedicated, I saw that she was standing behind the speaker. As he proceeded with the prayer she walked up behind him and seemed to merge with him. He faltered, as if trying to find the right words. Then, apparently more sure of what he was saying than before he paused, he continued. The words he spoke obviously were not the words he intended to say. He said later it was as if the words were being put in his mouth. I knew that was true, but I never told him how it was done. When the man who was offering the dedicatory prayer had said the things she wanted said, she stepped back away from him, then stepped forward and sprinkled something into the grave. With the dedication of the grave over, the family left.

I have treasured the other glimpses I have received when other family members have passed on. Sometimes I didn't see as much detail, but I always saw something from beyond the veil.

Grandfather Seen as a Younger Man

So it was when Georgia's grandmother and grandfather passed away. When George Weichers, Georgia's grandfather whom she was named after, passed away on March 22, 1976, at home in Magna, Utah, I saw him in the spirit world. I saw a different man than the one I was used to. He was much younger and didn't have the need for glasses. I saw him tending his beloved roses. How he took pride in his yard and his flowers before he died.

Since then my sister and father and my stepfather have all passed away. My son from my first marriage has also passed from this life.

In May of 1994 my mother, Edith Allison, also passed on. She suffered as a result of several strokes in the last years of her life. She struggled through a very trying time when she was forced to undergo a radical mastectomy because of cancer.

She also had Multiple Sclerosis. It was probably from this deteriorating condition that she suffered most the last few years of her life. In the end, as she fought for every breath, refusing to let go, I prayed and asked that she would be released and finally find the peace she never had in this life.

Felt Deceased Relatives Pass By

I was standing by the foot of her bed as she drew her last breath. Just at that moment I distinctly felt my step-father and sister brush past my arms, one on either side of me. I knew they had come to take her home. This was one of the few times I wasn't able to actually see anyone.

As much as I have seen and been involved in throughout my life, death still is a double-edged sword for me. Even though I have been there and have come back, and know what awaits myself and others when we pass over, the pain of losing someone is still very great. I am torn between this life and my vivid anticipation of life in the spirit world.

I do have the knowledge that all my loved ones that have crossed over have all found the truth to what I have professed concerning our next phase of existence all these years. I take solace in knowing that I will once again be with them some day.

Until then I will have to be content with my memories, and I'll always wonder how I will die the next time, and who will precede me. Will we have another family reunion then, like the last one, and will I get to stay there this time? Only God knows.

19

Final Thoughts and Observations

Protection and Guidance Received

As this book goes to press, it has been over twenty-five years since I had my accident. I have reflected back on my life on numerous occasions. I'm quite sure I have a guardian angel that is working overtime on my behalf. I have counted at least fifty different times that I should or could have died. Intervention by unseen forces has prevented tragedy, usually in the nick of time. These range from falls to surviving fire, to escaping drowning, and avoiding potentially fatal automobile accidents. The list goes on and on. Each time, I have felt an unseen force and realized from where the help came. I am glad for the help and realize that I am not alone in my struggles through this earthly life. I suspect that the protection and guidance I have received is typical of all of us. We are not alone as we pass through the tests of mortality.

Support From a Loving Spouse

Georgia has been my greatest inspiration. She never fails to encourage me to try new things. After the accident she didn't want to let me out of her sight at first; she was afraid that I might not come back. Over the years she has slowly relented, giving way to my fierce determination.

Georgia has helped our children through all the trials of growing up. They have achieved things they never knew were within their abilities. She has cultivated their latent talents, and she always has encouraged them to try harder.

Georgia's personality has been a cohesive element throughout our lives. Her own talents know no bounds, and she applies the same guidelines to her own life as those she has given to her family. Georgia's natural psychological abilities to discern the hidden nature of people and the interaction of their emotions has been a great blessing in our lives.

Our children are well adjusted and happy and have succeeded in their own right. They are now raising their own families. They are not without their own problems, but they have adopted Georgia's tenacity for resolving them.

We are the proud grandparents of sixteen grandchildren, ten boys and six girls. They are all special in their own right. Georgia happily spends every moment she can with them, not always as much as she would like, though.

Growth in My Profession

Just before my accident, I was scheduled to take the test to qualify as a journeyman electrician. After my accident, my doctor told me to plan on another occupation, one that would be better suited to my limited physical condition. I told him the only thing I ever wanted to be was an electrician. A little accident wasn't going to stop me. Two-and-a-half-years later I took a refresher course in the electrical code, reapplied, and took the state-sponsored test. My determination succeeded where common sense said I should have given up.

Working in construction has sometimes been very difficult, but I believe it has helped me to achieve the physical mobility I now enjoy.

Georgia's insistent persuasion helped me to go after and receive my master electrician's license and later my electrical contractor's license. I have been employed by Geneva Steel now over twenty years, and I have also built a modest contracting business outside of Geneva.

I don't recall the name of the company that we were remodeling the warehouse for. I do know that about five years after my accident, the building was taken over by Ampad Distributing. To date they are still in the building.

A Strong Testimony that Life Continues After Death

I have received a strong testimony to the continuation of our existence after we leave this mortal life. I might not have a complete understanding of the mysteries of God's plan of salvation, but I have a far greater comprehension now than I did before the accident. Many people have had slight out-of-body experiences and can attest to the peace and tranquility they felt. Many others have had more in-depth experiences and have returned to describe them in great detail.

From my near death-experience, I know with complete certainty that we have lived before in the pre-mortal existence as spirit intelligences, literal offspring of our Father in Heaven.

Increased Powers in the Life to Come

Because we are the children of our Father in Heaven, we have inherited many of his powers and abilities that we'll be able to use in the next phase of our eternal life. Among them are:

Powers of levitation or flying,

Ability to travel through space and time by thought,

Powers to communicate telepathically,

Participation in the eternal creation process, and

An eternal increase of knowledge, thereby intelligence and greater glory.

I also know that power and authority is delegated among God's offspring, and certain keys are given whereby we may have the authority to exercise those powers under God's direction and in his name.

Key Principles in God's Plan of Salvation

The plan of salvation that God has given us, whereby we might one day return and live in the celestial kingdom again, is just and divine.

For every law that God has decreed, there is a reward given for obedience and a consequence suffered for disobedience.

I have repeatedly been asked what I thought was the greatest lesson I have learned because of my experience. One of the most important lessons I received, I believe, is that we must learn to forgive ourselves, and we also must learn to forgive others.

Jesus Christ stated it differently, though I believe he was teaching the same thing, when he said we must first love God with all our heart, mind, might, and strength. And then we must love our neighbors as ourselves.

In order to love ourselves, we must first be willing to forgive ourselves. If God, our father, the greatest of all, can forgive us of even the most grievous sins, then we must learn to forgive ourselves too.

God Has Prepared the Way for Us

Being a just and loving Father, God has given us comforters and helpers to meet us when we leave this mortal sphere. I was comforted greatly by the being within the light after I passed through outer darkness when I left my body. I also was assigned a guide, someone I was comfortable with, to help me as I struggled to cope with my reentry into the spirit world.

I do know a great and wondrous existence awaits us, and that the central purpose of our earth life is to prepare ourselves to come and dwell there. And striving to perfect ourselves, both here and in the next phase of our existence, is the heart of that eternal purpose. We will grow as we return to the spirit world, and progress even more when we receive our resurrected bodies. And, hopefully, we will be able to enter into God's celestial city and presence. I know! I saw the after-death world of spirits, and I saw and sensed the eternal city—*I Saw Heaven!*

Publisher's Notes:
What Can Be Learned from This Account?

It's obvious to all who read it that I Saw Heaven! is a very extensive and profound report of many spirit-world activities, procedures and environments. To facilitate in-depth study of this account, 328 key statements have been identified and summarized or paraphrased in this section, which makes it a very comprehensive index of the concepts reported herein. The general topics are listed as they are first encountered in the book.

—Compiled by Duane S. Crowther

Souls in Outer Darkness, a Thick Foreboding Fog

1. Agonized souls floating in the fog, moaning and groaning, 56.
2. Emotions felt by those cast into outer darkness: pain, grief, eternal despair, frustration, misery, anguish and torment, 56.
3. The dark green fog was thick and almost black, 58.
4. The fog swirled and churned up to the entry into the spirit-world receiving room, 58.
5. The fog was repulsive, distasteful, very unpleasant, 58.

The Being in a Bright Light

6. Sensations felt in an out-of-body experience: warmth, overwhelming love, peace and joy, 40.
7. A brilliant white light, brighter than the sun and more intense, 56.
8. He was pulled toward the light, drawn very close, 56.
9. He could faintly see facial features in the light but nothing else, 56.
10. A soft, loving voice spoke from the light, 56.
11. He felt he was being comforted, 56.
12. He felt a peaceful calm, 56.
13. He felt unconditional love directed to him, 56.

The Life Review

14. The being in the bright light uttered a phrase which triggered a total recall of his life, 56.
15. His whole life passed before his eyes as if he was viewing a vivid film, 56.
16. The scenes were viewed at a very high speed, yet the speed seemed normal, 56.
17. Each scene was viewed with crystal clarity, 57.
18. He judged himself, 57.
19. There was no judgment felt from the being within the light, 57.
20. He felt unconditional, loving tolerance from the being within the light, 57.
21. He felt he had handled some situations well, 57.
22. He could see his spiritual development and advancement, 57.
23. He judged himself harshly for some situations, harder than any judge, 57.

24 He desperately wanted to go back and correct some of his actions, 57.
25. He saw some situations had retarded his spiritual development and held him back, 57.
26. He viewed everything at high speed, yet every scene was at a normal pace, 85.

The Stripping Away of Earthly Impurities

27. As his life review ended, the light from the being grew in intensity, 57.
28. The light burned through him with tremendous force, 57.
29. His body changed: earthly impurities were stripped away from it, 57.
30. Large areas of his body became transparent areas, 57.
31. He experienced no pain as the impurities and imperfections were stripped away, 57.
32. He felt tremendous exhilaration and elation as the stripping process ended, 57.
33. He felt free, no longer plagued by earthly imperfections, 57.
34. He recognized things we can't overcome on earth are burdens we carry all our lives, 57.
35. Some mortal burdens are so great they are carried into the spirit world, 58.

The Importance Of Self Forgiveness

36. The being within the light told him it was as important to forgive himself as to forgive others, 58.
37. Earth is a place for us to experiment and learn, 58.
38. Even God forgives our sins and mistakes, 58.
39. Not forgiving ourselves holds us back and keeps us from progressing, 58.
40. Fear of personal failure keeps us from trying anything, 58.

Feelings at a Parting View of Earth

41. He felt whole, complete, fully alive, 58.
42. He viewed earth from a great distance, 58
43. The earth looked like a small dirty brown tennis ball, 58.
44. He felt revulsion and was relieved and glad to be away from it, 58.

Unclothed at Entry into the Spirit World

45. He entered the spirit world naked, 59.
46. Two men clothed him in a white robe-like garment, 59.

The Entry Area and Facility

47. The arched doorway seemed suspended in space, 58.
48. An office at the end of the hall, 59.
49. A large desk, 59.
50. An old man with a long white beard wearing a robe, 59.
51. His name was written in a large book, 59.
52. Names of other men and women who had crossed over also were recorded, 59.
53. There is gender in the spirit world: men and women, 59.
54. Two benches of white and pink crystallized marble, 59.
55. Several doors, a room with a desk and pictures hanging on the wall, 59.
56. A street outside, 59.

His Guide

57. His features and physical appearance were more refined than on earth, 60.
58. His guide was assigned to him, 60.
59. The guide's roll: to reinstruct and reeducate until the entrant is familiar with his surroundings again, 60.

60. When I was finally admitted into the receiving room, I was taken on a tour just like the one I'm taking you on, 83.
61. Everyone is guided by someone he knew; it makes the transition easier, 83.

Telepathic Speech

62. His mouth doesn't move; his words are heard inside the head, 60.
63. It's one of the things you have to relearn, 60.
64. You'll hear both ways for a while, 60.
65. Everyone uses telepathy except those who have just crossed over, 60.
66. To communicate, you project out to that person, 77.
67. You can think out to an individual, to a group, or to everyone, 77.
68. When you're thinking to yourself your privacy is protected, 77.
69. Telepathy is the purest form of communication, 78.
70. If I sent a message telepathically about a place, you'd see it exactly as I saw it, 78.
71. You not only see what I see, you experience the emotions I feel, 78.

Senses Are Keener in the Spirit World

72. Acutely aware of everything, 60.
73. Senses feel as if increased a hundredfold, 60.
74. Again in possession of superior knowledge and intelligence withheld on earth, 60.
75. The veil is taken from your mind when you cross over, 60.
76. You soon regain all your powers and knowledge, 61.
77. It takes a little time and the right words to jog your memory, 61.

Returning Home to the Spirit World

78. Everything begins to look familiar, 61.
79. You have returned home, 61.
80. The buildings were becoming more familiar, 62.
81. Forgotten memories of meetings I used to attend were starting to surface, 63.
82. The council chambers—I thought things looked familiar, 63.
83. The council room had remained much the same since I was last there, 65.
84. If you go back to earth, the veil will probably drop across your mind again, 80.
85. There are things here you're not supposed to know, 80.
86. These things will be blocked for your own good, otherwise your free agency would be taken away, 80.
87. When your memory completely returns you'll see the perfect logic and harmony in all this, 83.
88. Memories of when we all were part of God's celestial world, 89.
89. He seemed to recall seeing some of these worlds before, 92.

Street and Buildings Described: a Small Community

90. Buildings along the street made of soft crystallized material, 61.
91. Buildings reflected different colors of a soft, subtle nature, 61.
92. The street is wide, 61.
93. A small town square, 61.
94. The center was about four city blocks, the town was several blocks wide, 61.
95. Most buildings were about four stories high, 61.
96. Some buildings were one and two stories high, 61.
97. A beautiful white two-story home with flowering plants, 83.
98. A spacious green lawn encompassed the house, disappearing into the trees behind, sidewalks in front, 83.
99. Many homes, manicured yards, set among large spreading trees, 85.

100. The trees appeared to go on forever, yet from the air we could see other homes right behind them, 85.

The Glory of God Described

101. A brilliant golden white light, almost like the sun, far down the street, 61.
102. Beautiful golden rays radiate in every direction, 61.
103. Every object glows when it reflects the rays, 61.
104. He felt all-encompassing brotherly love; secure and more loved, 62.
105. All children of Heavenly Father are linked through this love, 62.
106. A kinship with the universe through this universal spirituality and intelligence, 62.
107. Warm, vibrant feelings flood this love light, 62.
108. What you are seeing is the glory of God, 62.
109. The source of the light is God, 62.
110. His glory shines to the ends of his creations, 62.
111. The greatest of all his creations are his children, the greatest recipients of his love, 62.
112. I experienced again the same feelings of love and security . . . the pure essence of his love, 100.

Musical Ecstasy

113. He could hear music when looking at the light, 62.
114. He could feel the music vibrating through him, 62.
115. A haunting, melodic, musical symphony, 62.
116. Coming from every direction and every object, 62.
117. Sheer ecstasy from the sounds beautifully blended together, 62.

Attending Our Own Funerals

118. Everyone attends their own funeral, 63.
119. There are those we've left behind that need comforting, 63.
120. There will come a time when we need to know where our bodies are, 63.
121. We'll be reunited with our bodies as we become resurrected beings, 63.
122. It's a necessary part of our progression, 63.
123. When the family gathered at the viewing for the family prayer, he could see his mother-in-law's spirit standing beside the one giving the prayer, 141.
124. He also had a glimpse of her several hours before the funeral and could see her getting her hair done, and he observed how beautifully she was dressed, 141.
125. During the funeral she was there, moving from person to person. She stopped, bent forward, and kissed each one on the forehead, 142.
126. At the dedication of the grave, she was standing behind the speaker. During his prayer she walked up beside him and merged with him, 142.
127. The speaker's words obviously were not the words he intended to say. He said later it was as if words were put in his mouth, 142.
128. She stepped back away from the speaker, then stepped forward and sprinkled something into the grave, 142.
129. When Georgia's grandfather passed away, he saw him in the spirit world. He was much younger and didn't need glasses. He saw him tending his beloved roses, 142.
130. At the moment his mother died, he distinctly felt his step-father and sister brush past his arms. He knew they had come to take her home, 143.

Dying at Other Than the Appointed Time

131. You had a lot of years left; what happened to you was an accident, 64.
132. You're here before your time, 64.
133. Why were you not stopped and sent back before this?, 66.
134. Many people enter here by mistake and are sent back, but always before they get this far, 66.

The Death Decision

135. You're not dead yet; your body is still being kept alive on earth, 63.
136. A final decision hasn't been made yet, 63.
137. This will depend on you, 63.
138. If you decide to stay here, your body will cease to function, 64.
139. The only reason you still can go back is that your body can still sustain life, 64.

The Council Chambers

140. One-story tall, but taller than other single-story buildings, 65.
141. A large table in the center of the room, bookshelves against one wall, chairs, 65.
142. A council of twelve members, 65.
143. Still known by earth name: you're Larry, 66.

Pre-mortal Life Remembered

144. Memories of our pre-mortal life and the promises I had made were becoming more focused, 66.
145. I had made promises—that I would find her and take her through the temple, 67.
146. When you remember everything, then you'll understand all of Father's gospel doctrine, 73.

The Dangers of Returning to Mortality Known in the Spirit World

147. You'll be going back to a badly broken body, 68.
148. You'll experience unbelievable pain, 68.
149. You'll be subject to all the temptations of the flesh, 68.
150. We'll not interfere with your free agency, nor your children's, 68.
151. This experience will not make you unique or special, 103.
152. You will be subject to all the trials and temptations of the flesh, 103.
153. Unless you guard yourself carefully, you could still be led down to your own destruction, 103.

Travel by Flying: Levitation

154. Larry took me by the hand as we rose into the air, 69.
155. This is really a terrific way to travel, 74.
156. This is something you'll need to relearn, 77.
157. It's easier if I include you now [hold your hand]; later you'll be able to do it yourself, 74.
158. We came to a stop in the air about 20 feet from a group, 74.
159. Flying is a form of levitation, 78.
160. We're able to stand in the air without falling, 79.
161. We rose and began floating gently away, 91.
162. We gently soared above the heavenly landscape below, 91.

Landscape and Foliage Described

163. A large grove of trees, 69.
164. Trees around the genealogical research center, 69.
165. Low, tree-lined hills, 82.
166. Large trees like huge oaks lined the well-groomed street on either side, 82.

167. No weeds, trash or garbage of any kind anywhere, 86.
168. Wooded hills, placid lakes, gently gurgling streams, 92.
169. Parks, pavilions and stadiums dotted the landscape below, 92.
170. A large park with an entrance; the park was several hundred yards deep, 93.

The Genealogical Research Center

171. A beautiful white-domed building, 69.
172. Looked not too large from outside, but immense inside, 69.
173. Light and airy, high ceiling, large expansive windows, 69.
174. Divided in sections, long halls, 69.
175. High windows flanked by white-ribbed columns that arched to the ceiling, 70.
176. Large rooms with many shelves of books and manuscripts, 70.
177. Comfortable chairs and tables among the columns of books, 70.
178. A very large circular room with a high, ornately sculptured section, 70.
179. Many people were examining books and papers, 70.
180. This is one of our research centers, 70.
181. People are getting records and tracing their lines, 70.
182. From outside it appeared a normal-sized building, from inside it was immense, 85.

Ordinances Performed in the Spirit World

183. Without spirit-world genealogical data, ordinances can't be performed for people there, 70.
184. Performing [vicarious] ordinances on earth is only half of it; those same ordinances must be performed here to be complete, 71.
185. When vicarious ordinances are performed on earth, the people are under no obligation to accept them, 71.
186. If people do accept vicarious ordinances performed for them on earth, those same ordinances must be performed by the recipients in the spirit world to be binding, 71.
187. Everything on earth and in heaven goes hand in hand, 71.

Spirit-World Genealogical Research Linked to Research on Earth

188. Broken family lines [on earth] can be bridged by research that's done here, 71.
189. Family members here have often handed completed family records to someone on earth, 71.
190. If they do let you go back, would you please check on our family history lines?, 97.
191. We need to have the rest of our work done on earth before we can progress any further, 97.
192. I remembered their insistence as they instilled in me their desire to have their temple work done for them, 101.

The Power of Genealogical Links

193. The more links joined, the higher they were and the brighter they shone, 72.
194. Long golden chains were very high, and their combined light exceeded the sun's, 72.
195. Each person is a pure golden link possessing power and glory, 72.
196. As they became sealed, their combined power and glory increases, 72.
197. Sealing allows them to rise closer to the glory or perfection of God, 72.
198. Long family lines sealed together contain immense power, 72.
199. These groups are close to the celestial kingdom, 73.
200. Because of sealing, we'll someday share immortality and eternal life with Father, 73.

Learning Centers and Absorbing Knowledge

201. Four separate classroom groups seen, 74.
202. This is just one of the many learning centers here, 74.
203. Classes studying: taking notes, painting and sculpting, hearing lectures, 75.
204. Here everyone has a burning thirst for knowledge, 75.
205. One of the greatest joys here is the pursuit of knowledge, 75.
206. We have many different methods of learning, 75.
207. To learn about a book simply hold it; you can absorb the entire contents without opening it, 75.
208. By holding a book you can absorb the author's intent, feelings and emotions, 75.
209. We're able to absorb knowledge by touching, seeing or being close to something, 76.
210. Many things are transmitted telepathically, 76.
211. We absorb knowledge through every part of our bodies, 76.
212. Knowledge is useless without the experience to go with it, 76.
213. We get better the more we do it; perfection takes time, 76.
214. As we build on or perfect our talents, we're given other talents, 76.
215. Our knowledge and interests are expanding all the time, 76.
216. The greater our field of knowledge and experience, the more intelligent we become, 76.
217. If we're going to inherit Father's kingdom, we need to be intelligent enough to administer its affairs, 76.

Spirit Intelligence

218. What we are is spirit intelligence, 78.
219. We're governed by different laws and principles than other creations, 79.
220. The ideas and principles I've described don't usually apply to people on earth, 79.

Spirit-world Homes

221. A beautiful white, two-story home with flowering plants and green lawn, 83.
222. A middle-aged woman earned her home here through unselfish acts on earth, 84.
223. Earthly deeds of service are recorded in the spirit world, 84.
224. Each house was completely by itself, as if the house next door didn't exist, 85.
225. Each person's privacy seemed assured, 85.
226. Paradox: on one level things seemed normal size; from another view they seemed immense, 85.
227. Even though the homes were spaced evenly, each appeared completely isolated and alone, 85.
228. The home's surrounding yards offered privacy, like they were in the middle of a 40-acre field, 85.
229. Harmony and beauty are built into every creation here, 86.

Matter Exists at Different Vibrational Frequencies

230. Father s kingdom is governed by beauty and order, 86.
231. If men on earth lived as Father designed, then heaven and earth would actually become one, with no separation between them; the veil between would disappear, 86.
232. If men lived their lives right, they would elevate themselves spiritually and be able to see, 86.
233. All matter exists at certain vibrational frequencies, 86.
234. Spiritual or heavenly things vibrate at a higher frequency than earthly things, 86.

235. Their faster vibrations are why spiritual or heavenly things are invisible to those on earth, 86.
236. The more a man embraces evil, the more coarse he becomes. He vibrates at a lower frequency, 86.
237. The more spiritual a man becomes, the higher his vibrational frequency, 86.
238. Men can become so spiritual their vibrational frequencies become the same as heaven's; there is no separation between the two places, 86.

Aspects of Hell and Progression

239. Living in darkness, being cut off from Father's light, is pure hell for some, 87.
240. Always being able to see the best, but not being able to have it, also is hell, 87.
241. Progression is important because it allows us to accept and be part of the light, 87.
242. Father wants us to learn and accept his light, and to eventually become one with him, 87.
243. For most, being able to see what we were once part of, and not being able to obtain it again, would be hell, 90.
244. After seeing the Celestial city, to know I could never enter there would be an eternal hell for me, 91.

The Celestial City and Kingdom

245. A pale luminescence held my attention as we approached, 88.
246. At the base of the mountain lay a glorious city, 88.
247. Cliffs rose steeply, disappearing into a hazy mist. Very high mountains protruded through the mist, 88.
248. Light radiated, undulating from the pearlized buildings, 88.
249. A thousand different shades of color filled the spectrum, 88.
250. The sheer immensity of the city, 89.
251. Domed spires; each spire's dome was capped in pure gold, 89.
252. Pinnacles the color of platinum rose among the spines, 89.
253. Through each arched doorway and window shimmered a faint blue light, 89.
254. This is the Celestial Kingdom. From here, Father directs all the affairs of his creations, 89.
255. Only those very special spirits who have attained celestial status may reside there, 89.
256. The rest of us may only view it from a distance. It is out of bounds to us, 89.
257. Eventual perfection will afford us passage; until then we inhabit lower kingdoms, 89.
258. I can feel the utter divinity of the city, 89.
259. Of all the Father's creations, none can match the magnificence of the Celestial Kingdom, 90.
260. Is this God's home? Yes, 90.
261. Is this our Mother's home also? Yes, this is her home also, 90.
262. I can't bear to be within its sphere of radiance any longer, 91.
263. If you've not attained Celestial Glory, you can't exist in the Celestial Kingdom nor abide Father's glory unless he has changed you, allowing you to be in his presence without perishing, 96.
264. Father will not permit the unworthy to enter the Celestial Kingdom, 96.
265. Those of the higher kingdoms can visit the lower kingdoms, 96.

Other Worlds Without Number

266. Besides all you've seen, there are also other worlds to see and explore, 92.
267. There are worlds without number to satisfy the adventurous spirit in each of us, 92.

Family Reunions in the Spirit World
268. These are your relatives who lived on earth before you. They've all gathered to meet you and welcome you back, 93.
269. We wanted a reunion so we could meet you and let you get to know us, 96.
270. I was embraced fondly by each person. A panoramic view would flash through my mind of the experiences each individual had gone through. In this way I came to know each one intimately, 96.
271. I found how the family thread tied us together and learned my exact relationship to that person, 96.
272. The group wanted to know certain things about my family and what had been happening lately, 97.
273. If they do let you go back, would you please check on our family history lines?, 97.
274. We need to have the rest of the work done on earth before we can progress any further, 97.

Robes of Glory
275. Her long silky robe fluttered gently around her feet, 94.
276. Her robe shimmered with a radiance that dimmed the others around her, 94.
277. His entrant's robe seemed drab and gray by comparison, 94.
278. Don't be concerned, . . . your permanent robe will be given you later, 94.
279. Your permanent robe is being kept from you until they make a decision about you, 95.
280. My robe reflects the degree of glory I have obtained in the Celestial Kingdom, 96.
281. His robe hung halfway between his knees and ankles and was partially open down his chest, 102.
282. All these men were barefoot, 103.

We Return to the Spirit World as Adults
283. I was only three days old when I died. It was only necessary that I take a body. That's all the time I was given, 95.
284. When we die, we return here in adult form, just like before we were born, 95.

Spirit-world Time Is Faster than Earth Time
285. If you do go back, just remember that in a twinkling of an eye you'll be back here, 98.
286. Your time there will seem but a few moments to us. It really does pass by quickly, 98.

The Stadium
287. The stadium looked like a Roman Coliseum, 101.
288. The stadium was constructed in two semicircles, open at the ends, with tiered bleachers facing each other, 101.
289. The stadium was made of the same white, marble-like substance as the buildings, 101.
290. Twelve council members were seated to his left, another twelve to his right, 101.
291. In front of him was a six-foot-square marble platform about a foot high, 102.
292. Peter, James, and John described, 101-02.

Recollections of Pre-mortal Events
293. We had been together there for millennias of time before being sent to the earth, 66.
294. I saw myself when I had just been informed that my time to be born on earth had arrived, 126.
295. There was much to do and many preparations to make, yet little time to do it, 126.

Travel Through the Universe

296. I formed an image in my mind of where she was, 127.
297. I began moving with increased speed, 127.
298. In moments lights winked out as I broke the light barrier, 127.
299. Here and there a speck of light blinked on, then off as a star sped by, 127.
300. Time and space were no barriers, 127.
301. We had only to think of where we wanted to go and we would be there, 127.
302. Thoughts were faster then light, 127.
303. Suddenly, light flooded the universe again as my speed dropped. Ahead lay my destination as a speck before me grew in size, 127.
304. This speck quickly became a world as my speed continued to slow, 127.
305. I glided to a gentle stop under a large tree, 127.
306. We formed the image of our garden home in our minds, 128.
307. I held her hand tightly as we sped off, quickly exceeding the speed of light, 128.
308. The lights of the stars winked on and off as we sped through space, 128.
309. Just as quickly, our speed slowed, dropping us back into sub-light speed, 128.
310. A speck before us grew, quickly forming into a world as our speed continued to slow, 128.

Description of Another World

311. A beautiful rolling meadow of velvety green grass stretched out before me, 127.
312. Wild flowers of all descriptions and colors grew in splendid profusion, 127.
313. Large, stately trees offered shadowed light beneath their bows, 127.
314. The air was pure and vibrant, 127.
315. Rolling, sloping hills rose gently in the distance, 127.
316. Tiny children, numbering in the hundreds, were gleefully running about, 127.
317. The children played tag, danced in a circle, ran hand in hand, 127.
318. A beautiful glen by a stream. A soft, velvety green, mosey path followed the edge of the stream, 128.
319. Rolling hills ran in every direction, 128.
320. This will always be our garden, our special place. This was created for no one else but us, 128.
321. Magnificent trees surrounded the distant, misty hills, 130.
322. Water lilies bobbed in the water; beautiful flowers grew in stately splendor, filling the air with fragrance, 130.

Other-world Dress Styles

323. Her long, white dress hung gracefully from her right shoulder, leaving her left shoulder bare as the dress draped across her left breast. She was barefoot, 128.

Pre-Mortal Information about Earthly Births

324. How soon will you be leaving? They said the time was almost at hand, 129.
325. Have they said anything about me? Yes. [You will be born] very soon afterwards. In earth terms, probably just a couple of years, 129.
326. Geographically we'll be close, but it will probably be years before we find each other, 129.
327. I've made special arrangements here before we go over. When the time is right, we'll be down together, 129.
328. I'll make this promise to you now. After we're married and we complete all the necessary preparations, I'll take your through the temple and make you my queen, 130.

Index

About the Authors

I Saw Heaven! tells much of Larry and Georgia Tooley's life stories.

Larry several years before his accident.

Larry holds a master electrician's license and an electrical contractor's license. After working for twenty years for Geneva Steel as a maintenance electrician, he formed his own company, Rainbow Electric, and now devotes full time to that firm. Georgia also works in the company as general office manager. They have joined forces with a former coworker who is a general contractor, and they offer together a complete contracting package for their customers.

Larry today.

Larry's interests and hobbies include reading, driving and hiking in the mountains, and travel. He also enjoys writing and plans to continue his efforts as an author.

Larry and Georgia are living in Lehi, Utah. They are the grandparents of "16 wonderful grandchildren." Their children are located in Utah, California and Arizona.

Georgia today.